Saying Goodbye to a Beloved Pet

Understanding Pet Loss, Overcoming Guilt and Grief, Finding Peace, and Rediscovering Joy Again

Natalie Harlow

© Copyright 2024 - All rights reserved.

The content contained within this book may not be reproduced, duplicated or transmitted without direct written permission from the author or the publisher.

Under no circumstances will any blame or legal responsibility be held against the publisher, or author, for any damages, reparation, or monetary loss due to the information contained within this book, either directly or indirectly.

Legal Notice:

This book is copyright protected. It is only for personal use. You cannot amend, distribute, sell, use, quote or paraphrase any part, or the content within this book, without the consent of the author or publisher.

Disclaimer Notice:

Please note the information contained within this document is for educational and entertainment purposes only. All effort has been executed to present accurate, up to date, reliable, complete information. No warranties of any kind are declared or implied. Readers acknowledge that the author is not engaged in the rendering of legal, financial, medical or professional advice. The content within this book has been derived from various sources. Please consult a licensed professional before attempting any techniques outlined in this book.

By reading this document, the reader agrees that under no circumstances is the author responsible for any losses, direct or indirect, that are incurred as a result of the use of the information contained within this document, including, but not limited to, errors, omissions, or inaccuracies.

To my dear sister,

In memory of sweet Tripp, who filled your days with wagging tails and endless love. You gave him the world—treats, belly rubs, and all the cozy naps he could dream of. Though he's no longer by your side, may you find peace in the memories, warmth in the quiet moments, and strength in knowing that love never fades—it just transforms.

All my love

Table of Contents

INTRODUCTION 1

CHAPTER 1: THE HEARTBREAK OF LOSING A PET 5
    THE SPECIAL RELATIONSHIP BETWEEN HUMANS AND PETS 6
    ADDRESSING THE INITIAL SHOCK OF LOSS 8
    THE DIFFERENT KINDS OF PET RELATIONSHIPS 10
        Dogs 11
        Cats 11
        Small Pets 12
        Service Animals 13
    HOW THE LOSS OF A PET COMPARES TO HUMAN GRIEF 14
    GOODBYE, MY FRIEND 15

CHAPTER 2: WHY GUILT HAPPENS, AND HOW TO FORGIVE YOURSELF 19
    WHY GUILT OFTEN SURFACES IN PET LOSS 20
    Steps for Forgiving Yourself and Understanding Hard Decisions Don't Mean Failure 21
    Recognize That You Made Decisions With Love and Compassion 21
    Understand That Perfection Is Not Possible 22
    Separate Yourself From the Guilt of "What Ifs" 22
    Reframe Your Thoughts About Your Pet's Life 23
    Acknowledge That Saying Goodbye Is Always Hard 23
    Be Patient With Yourself 24
    HOW TO IDENTIFY GUILT TRIGGERS 24
    Practical Self-Forgiveness Techniques 25
    EXERCISES FOR REFRAMING YOUR THOUGHTS 27
    Gratitude Reflection 27
    Create a Memory Journal 27
    Talk Aloud to Your Pet 28
    Create a Ritual to Honor Your Pet 28
    Reframe Negative Thoughts With Positive Affirmations 28
    MY PERSONAL STORY 29
    The Day I Dreaded 30
    The Guilt That Followed 30

CHAPTER 3: GRIEF ISN'T LINEAR—WHAT TO EXPECT 33
    THE STAGES OF GRIEF 34

  Denial *34*
  Anger *35*
  Sadness *35*
  Acceptance *36*
 EMOTIONS IN THE GRIEVING PROCESS 36
  Grief Is Not a Straight Line *37*
  How Grief Changes Over Time and Why It's Important to Let It Unfold Naturally *37*
  Common Emotions in the Grieving Process *38*
  Tips for Self-Care When Grief Feels Overwhelming *39*

CHAPTER 4: MEMORIALIZING YOUR PET AND CREATING LASTING TRIBUTES .. 41

 WHY MEMORIALIZING YOUR PET CAN HELP WITH THE GRIEVING PROCESS 42
 CREATIVE WAYS TO MEMORIALIZE YOUR PET 43
  Writing Letters to Your Pet *44*
  Creating a Photo Album or Memory Box *44*
  Planting a Tree or Creating a Memorial Garden *45*
  Custom Art and Memorial Jewelry *46*
  Holding a Memorial Service *46*
 IDEAS FOR FAMILY AND COMMUNITY INVOLVEMENT IN REMEMBERING YOUR PET 47
  Family Involvement *47*
  Simple At-Home Ceremonies *48*
  DIY Projects to Honor Your Pet *48*

CHAPTER 5: THE PRACTICAL AFTERMATH—WHAT TO DO AFTER YOUR PET PASSES 51

 HOW TO HANDLE THE LOGISTICS AFTER A PET PASSES 52
  Immediate Steps to Take After Your Pet Passes *52*
  Deciding on Aftercare Options *53*
  Tips for Making Decisions Calmly *54*
  Resources for Finding Support *56*
  Legal Considerations *58*
 HOW TO TALK TO CHILDREN ABOUT WHAT HAPPENS NEXT 59
  Be Clear and Honest While Remaining Gentle *60*
  Encourage Questions and Be Ready to Answer *60*
  Validate Their Feelings *61*
  Involve Them in the Aftercare Process *61*
  Offer Reassurance for the Future *61*
  How to Talk to Loved Ones About What Happens Next *62*

CHAPTER 6: THE GUILT AROUND EUTHANASIA— RELEASING THE BURDEN 65

 WHY EUTHANASIA CAN FEEL LIKE A HEAVY BURDEN 66
  Talking to Your Veterinarian About Euthanasia Options *67*
 HOW TO SAY GOODBYE DURING THE EUTHANASIA PROCESS IN A MEANINGFUL WAY 68

THE DECISION-MAKING PROCESS 69
STORIES FROM OTHERS WHO FACED THIS DECISION AND HOW THEY FOUND COMFORT 69
AFTER-EUTHANASIA GRIEF AND HOW TO PROCESS COMPLEX EMOTIONS 70

CHAPTER 7: YOUR FAMILY (AND OTHER PETS) THROUGH GRIEF 73

HOW TO HELP CHILDREN UNDERSTAND AND PROCESS 74
   Grieving as a Family 74
   Explaining Death to Children in Age-Appropriate Ways 75
   Tips for Holding Family Conversations About the Loss 77
RECOGNIZING GRIEF IN OTHER PETS 79
   Behavioral Changes in Other Pets After a Loss, and How to Ease Their Anxiety 80
   Easing Anxiety in Grieving Pets 82

CHAPTER 8: REDISCOVERING JOY AFTER LOSS— HOW TO MOVE FORWARD .. 85

EMBRACING MEMORIES OF YOUR PET WHILE WELCOMING NEW JOY 86
HONORING YOUR PET'S LEGACY THROUGH ACTS OF KINDNESS OR ANIMAL ADVOCACY 87
FINDING JOY AGAIN 88
   Beginning to Think About Life After Loss 89
   Suggestions for Volunteering, Animal Welfare Work, or New Hobbies 89
   How to Talk About Your Pet's Life in Positive and Uplifting Ways 90
   Finding a Balance Between Holding on to Memories and Making Room for New Experiences 91

CHAPTER 9: FINDING HEALING IN NEW COMPANIONS (WHEN YOU'RE READY)93

WHEN AND HOW TO CONSIDER BRINGING A NEW PET 94
   When to Consider Bringing a New Pet Into Your Home 94
   Questions to Ask Yourself Before Adopting Another Pet 95
   How to Ensure Your Heart Has Space for Both the Memory of Your Lost Pet and the Love for a New One 96
EVALUATING YOUR EMOTIONAL READINESS FOR A NEW PET 97
   How to Choose the Right Time and Pet 98
   Practical Considerations 98

CONCLUSION 101

REFERENCES 107

Introduction

There's a quiet nook within each of us where memories curl up and make themselves at home—a place where the love for a pet resides. If you've ever looked into the trusting eyes of a pet and felt a connection, you understand the gravity of this loss. The sting of their absence dims the light of our routine and leaves a space that seems impossible to fill. Just looking at their favorite spot or catching a whiff of their scent on an old blanket can send ripples of grief through the hardiest of hearts. It is a unique and deep sorrow known well to those who have loved and lost an animal companion.

When people ask how you're doing, the words may catch in your throat. "It was just a pet," some might say, unintentionally dismissing the enormity of your loss. But your pet was a constant presence, an unspoken pillar of your daily existence. Your days were punctuated by feeding times, play sessions, or simply the comfort of their being nearby as you went about your business. They were the silent confidante—always waiting, always happy to see you—anchoring you through life's ebbs and flows.

That's the thing about pets—they become entwined in our lives in a sort of seamless symbiosis. They witness our private victories and defeats, sitting by our side through the mundane and the milestones. They offer a brand of companionship that's uncomplicated by the trappings of human interactions, pure in its intentions, and rich in consolation. When we face the void left by their departure, we feel like we are losing a fixture of our world—the kind that we thought was as permanent as the sunrise.

The grief is real. It reflects the bond you've nurtured, a measure of the countless moments of joy they brought into your life. Anyone who's loved a pet knows that the relationship is anything but trivial. So, let's talk about it, like two friends over coffee, unraveling the threads of loss and love, because this pain deserves a voice.

Pets never outstay their welcome. They do not dwell on our faults or remind us of our shortcomings. Instead, they bring with them an innocence and a purity of heart that is rare in our troubled world. We fuss over them, laugh at their antics, and, at times, confide in them better than we do with our human allies. Their absence leaves a silent echo that resonates through the halls of our hearts, disrupting the tune we've grown accustomed to.

You might find yourself expecting them to trot around the corner or to hear the familiar sounds of their movements. It's okay to listen for them, to miss the pitter-patter and the soft, comforting sounds. It's okay to look for them in their favorite sun spot or to set aside a piece of your meal for them unconsciously. These are the habits of love, the small rituals that make up the fabric of your shared lives.

That's because they never were "just pets"—they were part of the landscape of your home and a central character in the narrative of your life. Their quirks and habits, from the amusing ones that made you chuckle to the sometimes bothersome ones you came to tolerate fondly, all paint a picture completely irreplaceable.

Perhaps right now, the thought of coming home without being greeted by their excited presence or the comfort of their weight at your feet is unimaginable. There's an emptiness not just in the space they inhabited but in the routines you've built together. Their absence is palpable—a space once filled by a warm, living soul that shared your life without condition.

I remember the day like it was yesterday. Five years have passed, but the pain of losing my dog lingers as if time has only edged forward. That morning started just like any other, with his eager bark serving as my personal sunrise. It was a sunny day, and by evening, my world turned unexpectedly dark. My beloved companion, who had been struggling with health issues that we thought were improving, took a turn for the worse. The decision to let him go to avoid further suffering was the hardest choice I've ever had to make.

Let me tell you, in the simplest and most sincere of terms, going through the process of losing my dog was like losing my shadow. He'd followed me through countless life changes—moves, job shifts, and heartaches—always there, a reassuring presence. When he passed, it felt like a light went out. I'd look down expecting to see him beside me, but instead, there was just the cold floor. The silence in my home was deafening—no more click-clack of paws, no more soft whimpers or sighs of contentment as he slept.

In the aftermath, I was left alone performing our daily rituals. I'd reach out to fill his bowl at meal times, then pause, realizing his hearty appetite was no longer there to satisfy. His leash hung by the door, untouched and gathering dust, reminding me of the walks we no longer took. I found myself lost in a sea of memories that I clutched like a lifeline, and they also reminded me of what I had lost.

Processing my grief was a journey through an unfamiliar land. People tried to comfort me, offering well-meant but often hollow phrases like, "He's in a better place now" or "You can always get another dog." But he was my dog—my friend. And no one could ever replace him. Grief washed over me in waves, sometimes triggered by the smallest things like a dog barking in the distance, a toy hidden under the couch, or simply the way the sunlight flickered in a spot where he used to lay.

I took my time mourning because that's what he deserved. I allowed myself to feel the full weight of my sadness, to cry when the tears came, to laugh as I remembered the good times and the way he unapologetically took up so much room in my bed. I journaled, spoke openly with friends who understood, and some days, I just sat quietly with my memories.

This book is born out of my healing. I wanted to turn my experience, my story, into a lantern for others navigating the murky waters of pet loss. If you're reading this, maybe you're seeking a beacon to guide you through your own grief. I wrote these pages because I know the loneliness that comes with this process. It can feel as though you're speaking a language only you understand, and I don't want anyone to feel as isolated as I did.

My intent is to offer you companionship through these words. The wisdom in this book comes from research and a raw, heartfelt place. It's a concentration of the pain, the coping, and the eventual acceptance that shape a new normal after losing a pet.

Along the way, I discovered that grief is not a linear path. It's okay if one day you feel like you've moved forward, only to find yourself taking a step back the next. That's part of the journey. I've included insights drawn from the experiences of numerous others who have walked this bittersweet path.

The lessons I've learned and the experiences I've gathered are now shared with the hope that they will help you find your footing. It's my deepest wish that this book will be like a friend who sits with you—through the tender moments when you remember your pet's unconditional love to the times when you find the courage to forge ahead.

Chapter 1:

The Heartbreak of Losing a Pet

The bond between humans and their pets is something that's hard to put into words, yet so many of us know it well. A pet becomes a part of our everyday lives. There's something incredibly special about the way they greet us at the door, their tail wagging or their eyes lighting up as if they've been waiting all day just for that moment. It's in these small, often unnoticed moments that pets find a way to fill spaces in our hearts we didn't even realize were there.

For so many, the loss of a pet is heart-wrenching, like losing a piece of yourself. People sometimes don't expect the pain to hit as hard as it does, but when that constant, loving presence is suddenly gone, it leaves a deep, undeniable void. The grief that follows is not only real, but it can be just as profound as losing a human loved one. Pets offer us something so pure and uncomplicated—unconditional love and acceptance, no matter what we're going through. They don't judge, they don't hold grudges, and they're there, often silently, through life's toughest moments. So when that love and loyalty are no longer there, it can feel like the world has shifted in a way you weren't prepared for.

The shock of losing a pet can be overwhelming, and it's often so unexpected. Whether their passing was sudden or something you knew was coming, those first few days without them can feel like a blur of disbelief, sadness, and, at times, even guilt. You might catch yourself still looking for them in their favorite spot or expecting to hear the familiar sound of their paws on the floor. Your mind knows they're gone, but your heart just can't seem to accept it yet. These early emotions can be intense, and they tend to come and go in waves. Some days, you might feel numb, and other days, the sadness can be crushing. And that's okay—there's no right way to grieve.

What makes it even more difficult is that the bond we form with our pets is unique to each one. A relationship with a dog, with their boundless energy and loyalty, is so different from the quiet companionship a cat brings. The soothing feeling of watching a small pet, like a rabbit or a bird, brings its own sense of connection. And then there are service animals, who go beyond being companions—they're partners, offering critical support that's life-changing. Each relationship is one-of-a-kind, and so, too, is the grief when it comes to saying goodbye. It's not a pain that anyone else can fully understand because only you know the love and connection that was shared.

Losing a pet is often an invisible grief, one that others may not recognize or understand. People might offer kind words, but sometimes it's hard for them to see just how much your pet meant to you. The truth is, it's okay to feel the depth of your sadness, even if others don't quite get it. Just like losing a human loved one, the path to healing isn't straightforward. Some days will feel heavier than others, and there will be moments when a memory catches you off guard, and the tears come rushing back. But with time, the sharpness of the pain softens, and the memories of your pet start to bring smiles instead of tears.

There's something about hearing other people's stories of loss that can bring a small measure of comfort. Knowing that others have felt the same depth of sadness and have made it through to the other side offers a kind of hope. In sharing our stories, we realize that we're not alone in our grief and that, over time, the love and joy our pets brought us doesn't disappear—it transforms. It becomes a part of who we are, and it stays with us in the memories of their playful antics, the warmth of their presence, and the unspoken bond that lingers long after they're gone.

The Special Relationship Between Humans and Pets

The relationship between humans and pets is truly special. For many, it is about the deep emotional and social roles pets fulfill in our lives. Pets, whether they are dogs, cats, birds, or even smaller animals like rabbits, offer a type of companionship that is unconditional and pure. They do not judge us based on how we look, act, or feel on any given day. In fact, pets often seem to know when we need comfort the most, and their presence can be a source of tremendous emotional support.

One of the most important ways that pets fill emotional roles in our lives is through the sense of love and acceptance they provide. For instance, many of us feel pressures from our daily lives—from work, relationships, or other responsibilities. These pressures can sometimes make us feel unworthy or stressed. However, when we return home and are greeted by the wagging tail of a dog or the soft purr of a cat, it's hard not to feel a sense of relief. This is because pets offer a kind of love that is free from the complexities we often experience with other humans. They do not expect much from us other than our care and attention, and in return, they give us companionship and affection without hesitation.

Pets also play a crucial role in helping people cope with loneliness or isolation, especially those who live alone or the elderly, who may not have many social interactions throughout the day. For these people, a pet can be the lifeline that brings comfort and routine. Caring for a pet means that there is always someone to wake up to, feed, or simply talk to. It may sound simple, but these small interactions can be incredibly meaningful. For example, taking a dog for a walk can lead to conversations with other dog owners, creating opportunities for social engagement that may not have happened otherwise. In this way, pets help foster connections not just with their owners but also with others in the community.

Moreover, pets seem to have an intuitive sense of when their humans are feeling down. Many pet owners will tell you stories of how their dog or cat sat close to them during a difficult time, offering silent comfort. This is not a coincidence. Animals are highly attuned to their owners' emotional states, often responding in ways that provide exactly what their humans need at that moment. The simple act of petting a dog or cuddling a cat has been shown to lower stress levels and create a calming effect, which can be incredibly helpful during periods of sadness or anxiety (Wein, 2018). It is as if pets become emotional anchors, helping their humans navigate through the ups and downs of life.

In addition to emotional support, pets can also play a social role in our lives. As mentioned earlier, walking a dog often encourages social interaction with other pet owners, but the social benefits of having a pet extend beyond that. For instance, children who grow up with pets may develop stronger social skills and empathy. Pets teach children about responsibility, care, and emotional understanding. They learn to consider the needs of another living being, which can translate into stronger relationships with other people. Pets also help create a more vibrant home environment where laughter, play, and warmth are always present.

The special bond that forms between pets and their owners is, without a doubt, reciprocal. Just as pets provide us with emotional and social support, we do the same for them. Dogs, for example, thrive on routine and interaction. They benefit from daily walks, playtime, and human companionship, all of which contribute to their physical and mental well-being. Similarly, cats enjoy the comfort and security of a loving home where they can relax and interact with their owners at their own pace. This mutual relationship means that both pets and humans gain something valuable from their time together—whether it's a sense of purpose, companionship, or simply the joy of spending time with a friend.

Addressing the Initial Shock of Loss

When a beloved pet dies, the initial shock can feel overwhelming, leaving many people unsure of how to process their emotions. In the first few days, you might find yourself grappling with a range of feelings that shift from one moment to the next. The grief, for most, hits like a wave, and often it brings a sense of disbelief. Whether your pet's death was sudden or something you had anticipated, it doesn't always change how shocking it feels. There may be moments when it's hard to believe that your pet is really gone. You might even catch yourself calling for them out of habit, only to be painfully reminded that they're no longer there.

One of the first things you're likely to experience is a deep sense of emptiness. Pets, after all, are often a constant in our lives. They are there with us day in and day out, providing companionship, comfort, and a sense of routine. When they're suddenly no longer around, it's natural to feel like something crucial is missing. This emptiness can be especially hard during the times of day that were shared with your pet. These daily routines, which once brought comfort, can become sharp reminders of your loss.

Emotionally, the first few days after a pet's death can feel chaotic. There's often a mix of feelings that come in waves—in some moments, you might feel numb, unable to fully grasp what has happened, and in other moments, you may be consumed by sadness. It's not unusual to cry suddenly or feel completely overwhelmed, sometimes without warning. Many people find that their emotions shift unpredictably, making it difficult to get through even the simplest tasks. This unpredictability can feel exhausting, both mentally and physically, and it's important to recognize that this is a normal part of grief.

You may also find yourself feeling guilty, especially if you had to make the difficult decision to euthanize your pet. You might wonder if you did the right thing or if there was more you could have done to prolong their life. These feelings of guilt can be incredibly painful and can leave you second-guessing your decisions, even when you know deep down that you did your best to care for them. It's important to remember that guilt is a common part of the grieving process, especially when it comes to our pets because we feel responsible for their well-being.

In addition to guilt, some people experience a feeling of relief, particularly if their pet has been suffering. While it's natural to feel relief that their pain has ended, this can sometimes lead to additional feelings of guilt or confusion. "How can you feel relieved?" you might ask when you're heartbroken. It's important to understand that these conflicting emotions can coexist. Feeling relieved doesn't mean you loved your pet any less—it simply means you cared so much for them that you couldn't bear to see them in pain any longer.

Another emotion that often emerges in the early days is anger. You might find yourself feeling angry at the situation—angry that your pet had to suffer, angry that their life was cut short, or even angry at yourself for not being able to prevent their death. Anger can be a natural part of the grieving process, and though it may not make logical sense, it's important to allow yourself to feel it without judgment. Grief often brings a mix of emotions that are complex and difficult to untangle, and anger can be one of the ways your mind tries to process the depth of your pain.

For some, these intense feelings might also bring a sense of isolation. In the early days after losing a pet, you may feel as though no one truly understands what you're going through. It's not uncommon for others to offer well-meaning but dismissive comments, like "It was just a pet" or "You'll get over it soon." These kinds of remarks can make your grief feel minimized, leaving you feeling even more alone in your sorrow. It's important to seek out people who understand or to allow yourself space to grieve, knowing that your feelings are valid and that you are not alone in your pain.

During this time, it's also natural to revisit memories of your pet—both the happy ones and, at times, the difficult ones. You might find yourself looking through photos or remembering specific moments that bring tears to your eyes. This process of reminiscing is a way of holding on to the connection you had with your pet, and though it can be painful, it's also part of the healing process. It's okay to feel both sadness and joy as you think back on your time with them.

In these early days, self-compassion is key. Grief is not something you can rush through or avoid, and there is no "right" way to navigate it. You may need time to adjust to your new reality, and that's perfectly normal. Give yourself permission to feel the depth of your emotions, whether that's sadness, guilt, anger, or even moments of calm.

The Different Kinds of Pet Relationships

The relationships people develop with their pets are often very different depending on the type of animal they have, and these bonds can be just as varied as the pets themselves. Whether it's a playful dog, an independent cat, or even a small animal like a guinea pig, each type of pet brings something special to the lives of their owners. Because of this, the grief felt when they pass away can be quite unique to the kind of connection that was formed. In many ways, the role that each pet plays in someone's life shapes the depth and nature of the bond, which is why their loss feels so personal and profound. Let's explore the different kinds of relationships people might have with various types of pets.

Dogs

For many people, dogs are loyal companions and trusted confidants, and, more often than not, they feel like members of the family. The bond between a person and their dog tends to be built on daily routines that foster a deep connection. Dogs are known for being social creatures, and they thrive on interaction with their human companions. It's the way dogs offer comfort when we're feeling down, greet us excitedly when we come home, or curl up beside us on the couch after a long day. This sense of companionship, where the dog is by your side through both good and bad times, makes the relationship incredibly fulfilling.

Many dog owners feel that their dog is the one creature in the world who loves them unconditionally. This unconditional love can make the loss of a dog particularly painful because their presence brings a sense of security and happiness. Without them, there's often a noticeable emptiness in the home. For people who have had a dog for many years, the grief can be intense because the pet has been there through major life changes—relationships, jobs, health issues—and has always provided a constant source of comfort. Losing a dog is like losing a best friend, and that kind of bond is hard to replace.

Cats

Cats, in contrast to dogs, are often seen as more independent animals, but that doesn't mean the bond between a cat and its owner is any less meaningful. Cats may not be as outwardly affectionate or as constantly present as dogs, but they have a special way of connecting with their humans that often feels profound. Cats often show their love in subtle ways, like rubbing against you, purring in your lap, or quietly following you around the house. They tend to be more reserved in how they interact, but the moments they choose to seek out your attention are deeply appreciated.

One of the beautiful things about cats is their ability to provide a sense of calm and comfort without needing to be overly demanding. Many cat owners find solace in their cat's quiet presence, whether it's the soothing sound of their purring or simply having them curled up nearby. Because of this, the loss of a cat can feel especially emotional during quiet moments when their absence becomes most noticeable. For people who live alone or have relied on their cat for emotional comfort, the grief of losing such a calm and constant companion can be overwhelming.

Cats also have long lifespans, often living for over a decade, which means they are there for significant parts of their owner's life. When they pass away, it's not uncommon to feel like a part of your daily life is missing. Their loss can bring an emptiness that's hard to fill, as they were likely a source of both companionship and emotional comfort.

Small Pets

Small pets, such as rabbits, guinea pigs, hamsters, and birds, might not seem as significant to some, but to their owners, these animals can offer just as much love and companionship as larger pets. While they may not be as involved in your day-to-day routines as a dog or cat might be, small pets often bring moments of joy and delight through their quirky behaviors and gentle presence. They might not follow you around the house, but their personalities are often endearing in different ways—the way a rabbit hops excitedly for treats or the soft chirping of a bird that fills your home with life.

For children, in particular, small pets are often their first experience of having a companion animal. The bond that is formed through caring for these pets, feeding them, and cleaning their cages helps teach responsibility and empathy. When a small pet dies, the grief can be especially hard for younger family members, as it may be their first experience with loss. Even for adults, the passing of a small pet can be unexpectedly difficult. These animals might have been part of your daily routine, and though their presence was small, the emptiness they leave behind can feel quite large.

While small pets may have shorter lifespans, the emotional bond formed with them is no less significant. People often talk about how these little creatures bring joy in the simplest of ways, and their loss can feel like a big piece of that happiness is gone.

Service Animals

Service animals hold a particularly unique and important place in the lives of their owners. Unlike pets that are purely for companionship, service animals—such as guide dogs, hearing dogs, or therapy animals—are trained to perform tasks that help their owners navigate daily life (Brennan, n.d.). For people with disabilities or emotional challenges, a service animal provides not only emotional comfort but also physical support and independence. This special relationship goes beyond a typical pet-owner dynamic, as service animals are trusted partners who assist in maintaining the safety and well-being of their owners.

The bond with a service animal is often incredibly strong because these animals are lifelines. They accompany their owners everywhere, ensuring they can live independently, perform daily tasks, and even manage emotional challenges. When a service animal dies, the loss can feel twofold: not only is there the emotional pain of losing a beloved companion, but there is also the practical loss of the support they provided. For someone who has relied on a service animal for years, their absence can create a feeling of vulnerability and uncertainty about how to cope without that level of assistance.

In this case, the grief can also be accompanied by a deep sense of appreciation for all the ways the animal helped. Service animals are incredibly loyal and dedicated to their work, and when they pass, it can feel like losing a partner who was always there to help carry the weight of everyday life.

How the Loss of a Pet Compares to Human Grief

Many people are often surprised by the intensity of their grief. It may feel as though the pain is just as deep or even deeper than what they've experienced with human losses. This can be confusing, and at times, it can even lead to feelings of guilt—people may wonder why they are grieving so intensely for an animal. But the truth is, the bonds we form with our pets are incredibly strong and unique, and in many ways, they can mirror, or even exceed, the depth of human relationships.

One of the main reasons the loss of a pet can feel as painful as human grief is the level of emotional support pets offer. Pets are often with us every day. Their unconditional love and loyalty create a safe space for us to be ourselves without fear of judgment.

It's important to note that pets hold an emotional place in our lives. For example, many people describe their pets as being there for them in ways that people aren't always able to be. Pets offer nonverbal communication, and it's this silent companionship that often makes their absence so hard to process. You may have shared intimate, quiet moments with your pet—moments when they seemed to sense your emotions and simply stayed by your side without needing words. It's these small but deep connections that deepen the grief when they are no longer there.

Another factor to consider is the level of care and responsibility that comes with being a pet owner. Unlike most human relationships, where we care for each other in various ways, pets are often entirely dependent on us for their well-being. We are responsible for feeding them, ensuring their health, and providing them with love and attention. This creates a deep sense of attachment and, with it, a strong sense of responsibility.

In addition to the personal emotional pain, the societal response to pet grief can make the experience even more isolating. While losing a human family member or friend is often met with an outpouring of support and acknowledgment, the loss of a pet may not receive the same level of validation. People may not fully understand the depth of your grief, and well-meaning comments like "It was just a dog" or "You can always get another pet" can feel dismissive and painful. This lack of societal recognition for pet loss can leave you feeling alone in your grief, adding to the emotional weight you're already carrying.

In fact, this societal gap in understanding pet grief can contribute to what is known as "disenfranchised grief." This term refers to grief that is not openly acknowledged or socially supported. When the emotional pain of losing a pet is not recognized by those around you, it can make the grieving process more challenging. You may feel pressured to move on quickly or suppress your feelings, even though you are deeply mourning the loss of a beloved companion. In contrast, when we lose a human loved one, there are often formal rituals like funerals or memorials that help provide closure and allow space for shared mourning. The absence of such rituals for pets can make the grieving process feel even lonelier.

Goodbye, My Friend

One story that truly touches the heart and shows how deeply people can grieve the loss of their pet comes from Jackie Buckle. Jackie lost her beloved cat, Max, and her experience not only highlights the pain of losing a pet but also how that grief can eventually lead to healing.

Max was a beautiful tuxedo cat known for his soft green eyes and those long whiskers that stood out like piano wires. He was always nearby, following Jackie around the house with his loud, chirpy meow. Although Max wasn't one to sit in her lap for long, Jackie cherished the moments when he would let her hold him for just a few seconds before he wriggled free. He had a strong presence in Jackie's life.

One day, Jackie noticed that Max wasn't quite himself. He seemed quieter than usual, more tired. At first, she didn't think too much of it. But when Max began panting heavily later that day, her worry grew, and they rushed him to the vet. It was during that visit that Jackie received the heartbreaking news: Max had congestive heart failure. This marked the beginning of weeks of vet visits and medical procedures, all in the hope of saving Max.

Despite his condition, Max remained as feisty as ever. He disliked the trips to the vet and would struggle whenever Jackie tried to put him in his carrier. Even though his health was declining, Max still had that spark of defiance that made him unique. However, as time went on, it became clear that Max was not going to get better, and Jackie had to make the incredibly difficult decision to let him go.

After Max's passing, the house felt empty. Jackie could feel the absence of her cat in every corner. She missed the little routines they shared, the simple joy of having Max nearby as she worked from home. Her daughters, who also loved Max, tried to help her cope. They would take her out for coffee, patiently listening as she talked about how much she missed him. But since Jackie worked from home, it had often just been her and Max during the day, making the loneliness even harder to bear.

In search of comfort, Jackie turned to the internet, where she found the Blue Cross pet memorial wall. Reading the many heartfelt tributes left by others who had lost their pets brought her some relief. She realized that she wasn't alone in her grief, and it encouraged her to write her own tribute to Max. This act of remembrance helped her feel connected to him, giving her a way to honor his memory.

As the months passed, Jackie slowly came to terms with Max's absence. She made a little photo montage of him, and every day she would touch it. While at first the sight of his pictures brought tears and feelings of regret, over time, Jackie began to smile when she looked at them. She remembered the joy Max had brought to her life—the way he was so feisty and full of character. She realized just how lucky she had been to share her life with him.

Eventually, Jackie felt a desire to help others who were going through the same pain she had experienced. She became a volunteer for Blue Cross Pet Loss Support, offering a listening ear and words of comfort to those struggling with the loss of their pets. Jackie found that many of the people she spoke with shared similar feelings—the strong bonds they had with their pets and the deep sense of loss they felt afterward.

For Jackie, the journey from grief to healing wasn't easy, but she found that by sharing her story and listening to others, she could help people feel less alone in their pain. Through her experience, Jackie shows that while the grief of losing a pet is intense, the love and memories they leave behind are just as powerful (Blue Cross, n.d.).

This story is based on the real-life account of Jackie Buckle, shared through the Blue Cross Pet Loss Support program.

Chapter 2:

Why Guilt Happens, and How to Forgive Yourself

Losing a pet is such a deeply emotional experience, and it's often filled with a wide range of complicated feelings. Among these, guilt tends to come up quite frequently. Many people find themselves constantly questioning their actions, wondering whether they made the right choices or if maybe they could have done something differently. Whether it comes from difficult decisions like euthanasia, unfortunate accidents, or illnesses that might have seemed preventable, guilt can really start to feel like a heavy burden during the grieving process.

It's completely natural for guilt to show up when we lose a beloved pet, especially since our pets rely on us so much for their care and well-being. We might find ourselves thinking back to moments where we believe we should have done more or we wish we had made different choices, and these thoughts can often stay with us, making the loss feel even more painful. However, it's really important to remember that making those difficult decisions for our pets doesn't mean we failed them in any way. In fact, it actually shows just how much love and care we had for them and the enormous responsibility we took to ensure their comfort and safety.

Forgiving yourself can certainly feel like a challenge, especially when guilt starts to cloud the memories of all the good times you shared with your pet. But by taking some steps to better understand these feelings, you can begin to release the guilt and instead focus on the love and care you provided. Self-compassion plays a crucial role in this process, allowing you to honor the special bond you had with your pet without being weighed down by feelings of regret or those endless "what-ifs."

There are definitely several ways to start this journey of self-forgiveness. Taking time to reflect on your emotions, figuring out what exactly triggers the guilt, and practicing kindness toward yourself can all make a significant difference. For example, writing letters to yourself or even to your pet can be a powerful way to release those emotions. It gives you the chance to express your love and sorrow while also helping you shift the way you see your actions and the choices you make.

Why Guilt Often Surfaces in Pet Loss

When we lose a pet, especially under difficult circumstances like euthanasia decisions, accidents, or preventable illnesses, it's common for feelings of guilt to surface. Guilt comes from our deep sense of responsibility toward our pets and the love we have for them. Pets rely on us entirely for their care and well-being, which often makes us feel accountable for every aspect of their lives, especially when things go wrong.

In the case of euthanasia, guilt often arises because we are making the decision to end our pet's life. Even though euthanasia is a compassionate choice to relieve suffering, it can feel like we are playing an active role in their death, which weighs heavily on our emotions. We might question if we made the decision too soon or waited too long, wondering if we robbed them of more time or allowed them to suffer unnecessarily.

Accidents and preventable illnesses trigger guilt because we feel that we should have been able to stop these situations from happening. It is easy to fall into the trap of believing that if we had done something differently, we could have changed the outcome. For example, we might think, "If only I hadn't left the door open," or "If only I had noticed the signs of illness earlier."

Steps for Forgiving Yourself and Understanding Hard Decisions Don't Mean Failure

Forgiving yourself after the loss of a pet, especially when you've had to make hard decisions like euthanasia or dealing with preventable illnesses, is one of the most important steps in the healing process. It's also one of the most challenging because we tend to be our own harshest critics. When we lose a pet, especially after making a life-altering decision for them, it's natural to question ourselves. We wonder, *Did I do the right thing? Could I have done more?* These thoughts can be overwhelming, but it's essential to remember that hard decisions, especially those made with love, do not mean you've failed your pet.

Recognize That You Made Decisions With Love and Compassion

One of the first steps in forgiving yourself is to acknowledge that every choice you made for your pet was rooted in love and a desire to do what was best for them. Whether it was the decision to pursue treatment or the heartbreaking decision to let them go, your motivation was to alleviate their pain or improve their quality of life. It's easy to forget this when guilt clouds our thoughts, but taking a step back and remembering that your choices were made from a place of love can help shift your perspective.

For example, euthanasia, although it may feel like an impossible choice, is often the kindest thing we can do when a pet is suffering. It allows them to pass peacefully without prolonged pain or discomfort. While it's normal to feel conflicted about the timing or the decision itself, it's important to remind yourself that this choice was an act of compassion, a final gift you gave to your pet. Many people struggle with this decision, but it doesn't diminish the care and love you provide throughout your pet's life.

Understand That Perfection Is Not Possible

No pet owner is perfect, and that's okay. We often put immense pressure on ourselves to be the perfect caregivers, but the reality is that life is unpredictable, and no one can foresee every possible outcome. It's common to look back on your pet's life and think *If only I had done this differently*, but the truth is, you made the best decisions you could with the information you had at the time. Hindsight can make us feel like we should have known better, but it's important to accept that we can't predict the future or control every situation.

Think of all the times you did something good for your pet, all the love you gave them daily, and how you enriched their life. That's what matters in the long run—not the mistakes we believe we made. By embracing the fact that perfection is unattainable, you can start to release the pressure you're putting on yourself and focus on the bigger picture: the life of love, joy, and companionship you shared with your pet.

Separate Yourself From the Guilt of "What Ifs"

The "what ifs" that come after losing a pet can be paralyzing. *What if I had noticed their illness sooner? What if I had tried one more treatment? What if I had waited another day?* These thoughts feed into feelings of guilt, making you believe that you could have prevented your pet's death if only you had acted differently. But these "what if" questions often arise from hindsight bias, which makes it seem like things were clearer at the time than they actually were. In reality, you didn't have the ability to see how everything would unfold, and you did your best with the knowledge you had.

One way to deal with these "what if" questions is to remind yourself that they are based on emotions, not facts. In moments of grief, it's easy to get lost in hypothetical scenarios, but it's important to ground yourself in what is real. You made choices that you believed were right at the time. When guilt comes from imagining different outcomes, take a deep breath and remind yourself that you acted with the information available to you then, not the information you have now.

Reframe Your Thoughts About Your Pet's Life

Another step toward self-forgiveness is to focus on the whole of your pet's life rather than fixating on their final days. It's natural to concentrate on those last moments because they're fresh and emotionally charged, but doing so can overshadow the many years of happiness and love you shared. Ask yourself: *Did my pet know love? Did I make them feel safe and happy?* The answer to those questions will almost always be "yes," and that's what truly matters.

Try to think of your pet's life as a journey filled with good times—playful moments, quiet cuddles, walks in the park, or those simple, everyday moments when they were just happy to be with you. This reframing of your thoughts helps you see that while the end of their life was difficult, it was only a small part of a much larger story. By focusing on the joy you brought them and the love they felt, you can start to soften the edges of your guilt.

Acknowledge That Saying Goodbye Is Always Hard

It's essential to recognize that no matter when or how you say goodbye to a beloved pet, it's always going to be hard. There is no "perfect" time, and there is no "right" way to do it. Many people struggle with the question of whether they made the decision too early or too late, but in the end, what matters is that you were there for your pet when they needed you most. You provided them with care, love, and, ultimately, peace.

It's important to remind yourself that even if you question the timing of your decision, it doesn't change the fact that your intention was always to do what was best for your pet. It's natural to feel conflicted about it, but over time, you'll come to see that you made a compassionate choice out of love.

Be Patient With Yourself

Forgiving yourself is not something that happens overnight. It's a gradual process that requires patience and self-compassion. You may have days when the guilt feels overwhelming, but there will also be days when you feel more at peace with your decisions. Allow yourself to move through these emotions at your own pace without pressuring yourself to "get over it" quickly.

Understand that grief and guilt are normal reactions to the loss of a pet, and they don't diminish the love you had for your companion. By giving yourself the time and space to grieve, you are also allowing yourself to heal. Self-forgiveness is part of that healing process, and it begins with accepting that you did the best you could, even when faced with incredibly difficult decisions.

How to Identify Guilt Triggers

Guilt triggers are specific thoughts, situations, or memories that bring up feelings of guilt. These could be moments when you recall the decisions you made about your pet's care or when something reminds you of your pet's final days. You might find yourself thinking about the exact time you chose euthanasia or reliving a moment when you felt you should have acted differently.

To identify these triggers, pay attention to when the feelings of guilt arise. Do they happen when you see a photo of your pet? Or when you drive by the veterinary clinic? By recognizing these moments, you can prepare yourself to handle the emotions that follow.

It is also common to feel guilt when you think about how happy your pet was before they became sick or injured. Comparing those happy memories to their final moments can create a painful contrast, making you question whether you did enough to preserve their happiness. It's important to understand that these thoughts are natural but not a reflection of your love and care.

Practical Self-Forgiveness Techniques

Self-forgiveness is an essential part of healing after the loss of a pet, but it can be hard to know where to start. We tend to be harder on ourselves than anyone else, and when grief is involved, those feelings of guilt and self-blame can intensify. However, there are specific techniques you can use to help move toward forgiveness. These practices are not meant to make the pain disappear overnight, but they can guide you toward letting go of unnecessary guilt and allowing yourself to heal.

Practice Self-Compassion

The first step is to treat yourself with the same kindness and understanding that you would offer a friend in your situation. Imagine if a close friend came to you, heartbroken over the loss of their pet and filled with guilt. Would you judge them or criticize their decisions? Most likely, you would offer them comfort, reminding them that they did their best and that their pet was loved deeply. Now, try to turn that same compassion inward toward yourself.

It's important to acknowledge your feelings without judging them. Feeling guilt doesn't mean you are guilty of wrongdoing—it's simply a natural part of grief. Tell yourself, "I'm allowed to feel this way, but it doesn't mean I've done something wrong." By being gentle with yourself, you allow room for healing and acceptance.

Write a Letter to Yourself

Writing can be a powerful way to process the complex emotions that come with losing a pet. One effective technique is to write a letter to yourself. In this letter, express the guilt, sadness, and regret you may be carrying. It might feel difficult to put these feelings into words, but it can be incredibly cathartic to see them written down. Be honest about what you're struggling with.

Once you've expressed your feelings, take a moment to write another letter—this time from the perspective of your pet. Imagine what they would say to you if they could. Pets don't hold grudges, and they don't expect perfection. In this letter, let your pet remind you of the love you gave them and the joy they experienced because of you. It's a way to release some of the weight you may be carrying and shift your perspective from guilt to gratitude.

Reframe the Narrative

When we lose a pet, it's easy to let the final days or moments define the entire relationship we had with them. However, one of the most important self-forgiveness techniques is to reframe this narrative. Instead of focusing solely on the difficult decision you had to make, try to see the bigger picture of your pet's life.

For instance, remind yourself of the happy times—those moments of pure joy and love that made your bond so special. Did your dog greet you at the door every day, tail wagging with excitement? Did your cat curl up next to you in bed, purring contentedly? Those moments are just as much a part of your pet's story as the final days. Shifting your focus to positive memories helps balance the weight of grief and makes it easier to forgive yourself.

Acknowledge the Challenges You Faced

Another way to move toward self-forgiveness is by acknowledging that you were faced with incredibly difficult choices. Whether it was the decision to euthanize, dealing with a preventable illness, or managing an accident, none of these situations come with easy answers. It's okay to recognize that the decisions you made were hard. There's no perfect solution at these moments, and doing the best you can with the information and resources available at the time is all anyone can ask of you.

Exercises for Reframing Your Thoughts

Letting go of guilt is a process, and part of that process involves changing the way you think about your pet's life and their passing. Reframing your thoughts helps you shift from focusing on guilt to remembering the love and happiness your pet brought into your life. Here are a few exercises you can practice to start reframing your thoughts and healing from the loss.

Gratitude Reflection

Gratitude is a simple but powerful tool for reframing how we see the world—and, in this case, how we view our relationship with our pet. Take a few moments each day to reflect on the things you are grateful for when it comes to your pet. Write them down if that helps. You might think of little things, like the way they looked at you with unconditional love, or bigger moments, like the way they helped you through difficult times.

This practice shifts your focus away from guilt and regret and toward the positive impact your pet had on your life. By focusing on gratitude, you remind yourself that your pet's life was filled with love and joy, which helps ease the weight of guilt.

Create a Memory Journal

A memory journal is another way to honor your pet and reframe the way you think about their life. Instead of fixating on their last days, fill this journal with stories, memories, and moments that made your time together special. Write about the funny quirks they had, the way they played, and the times they comforted you. Add photos, drawings, or mementos if you'd like.

Whenever guilt starts to creep in, return to this journal. Reading about the happy times will remind you that your pet's life was much more than its ending. By celebrating the memories, you'll start to see their life as a whole rather than focusing on their passing.

Talk Aloud to Your Pet

Talking to your pet even after they've passed can be surprisingly comforting. It's a way to express your feelings, both sadness and gratitude, in a space where you feel connected to them. You can do this in the privacy of your home or in a special place where you feel close to your pet.

You might start by simply telling them how much you miss them and how sorry you feel for any guilt you're carrying. Then, shift the conversation to remembering the good times. Tell them about the joy they brought into your life, and thank them for the love they gave. This simple exercise can help you feel a sense of closure and peace.

Create a Ritual to Honor Your Pet

Sometimes, performing a small ritual can help reframe the way you view your pet's life and passing. This might be something as simple as lighting a candle in their memory each evening or planting a tree or flower in their honor. If you have your pet's ashes, you could choose a special place to scatter them or keep them in a memorial box.

These small acts of remembrance provide a way to express your love and honor your pet's memory rather than focusing on the guilt. They give you a tangible way to connect with the positive aspects of your relationship and help create a sense of peace.

Reframe Negative Thoughts With Positive Affirmations

When guilt surfaces, it's often accompanied by negative self-talk. Thoughts like *I didn't do enough*" or *I should have made a different decision* can quickly take over. One way to counteract these thoughts is by using positive affirmations.

Each time you catch yourself thinking a negative thought, consciously replace it with a positive affirmation. For example, if you think, *I didn't do enough*, replace it with, *I gave my pet a life full of love*. Or, if you find yourself thinking, *I made the wrong choice*, counter it with, *I made the best choice I could with love in my heart*. Over time, these affirmations can help shift your mindset and allow you to let go of guilt.

My Personal Story

Losing a pet is one of the hardest things I've ever gone through. It's not something you can ever really prepare for, even though, as pet owners, we all know that day will eventually come. The bond we form with our pets goes beyond words, and when they're gone, it leaves an emptiness that is difficult to describe.

In my case, I had Oliver, a wonderful dog, for over 17 years. We went through so much together—he was there during some of the toughest times in my life. From dealing with personal challenges like anxiety and depression to being by my side through all of life's milestones, he was my constant companion. But with that closeness came an intense sense of responsibility, and when Oliver's health started to decline, so did my ability to avoid feelings of guilt.

Oliver was like family to me. I had always wanted a dog, and when I finally got him for my 10th birthday, it was like a dream come true. He was exactly the kind of dog I had always imagined—white with black patches, just like the ones I used to draw when I was younger. From the moment we brought him home, we were inseparable.

Oliver saw me through everything—school, health struggles, family difficulties—and always seemed to know when I needed comfort. He had this quiet presence that made everything a little bit better, even on the hardest days. As the years went on, we grew older together, and though his health started to show signs of aging, he was still full of life. He was tough—surviving pancreatitis and even going nearly blind in his later years without much trouble. For the longest time, I thought he would live forever, or at least, I hoped he would.

It wasn't until Oliver was about 17 years old that I started to notice more frequent health issues. He would catch little bugs here and there, but the vet couldn't pinpoint anything major. In my heart, I think I knew he was starting to slow down, but it was difficult to accept. I didn't want to believe that my time with him was running out.

In September 2019, my mom gently told me to prepare myself, suggesting that it might be his last Christmas with us. At first, I couldn't accept it. I cried and even accused her of giving up on him. But deep down, I think I knew she was right. Still, I wasn't ready to face the reality of losing him.

The Day I Dreaded

In November 2019, things took a turn. One night, Oliver started vomiting blood, and his energy just wasn't there anymore. It was heartbreaking to see him like that. We knew we had to take him to the vet the next morning, but waiting for that appointment was agonizing. I kept hoping, deep down, that there might be another treatment or that maybe he could pull through like he had so many times before. But when we finally made it to the vet, it was clear that his time had come.

I had never felt so conflicted in my life. The vet confirmed what I feared—there was nothing more they could do. Making the decision to euthanize him was the hardest thing I've ever done. Even though I knew it was the kindest option, knowing that I had to let him go was unbearable. I was filled with guilt, feeling as though I was giving up on my best friend when he needed me the most.

The Guilt That Followed

After Oliver passed, I was flooded with feelings of guilt. I replayed those last moments over and over in my mind, questioning everything. *What if we had tried harder? What if I had caught the signs sooner? What if there was something more we could have done?* It was like my mind wouldn't let go of the idea that I could have somehow changed the outcome. I even felt guilty about the timing of his euthanasia, wondering if we waited too long or acted too soon. It's a feeling I wouldn't wish on anyone, but it's all too common after losing a pet.

I also felt a sense of guilt in the way I grieved. I thought I was making things harder for my family by being so emotional, even though they were going through their own grief, too. On top of that, I worried about moving on without Oliver, as if doing so would mean betraying his memory.

It took time, but I began to realize that guilt was a natural part of my grief and that I needed to work through it. One thing that really helped me was trusting the advice of our vet. They reassured me that there was nothing more we could have done for Oliver, and I needed to hear that. It reminded me that we had made the best decision we could for him out of love and concern for his well-being.

I also had to come to terms with the fact that the guilt I was feeling wasn't an indication that I had failed Oliver. Instead, it was a reflection of how much I loved him. Guilt is often tied to our desire to protect the ones we love, and that's what it was for me. I wasn't guilty of anything—I just cared so deeply about Oliver that I wanted to have done everything perfectly, which is impossible.

The most important lesson I learned from this experience was that the love I gave Oliver throughout his life far outweighed any feelings of guilt I had after his passing. I had to remind myself of all the years of happiness, the walks, the moments of comfort, and the way we were always there for each other. When I think about his life as a whole, I know he was happy, and that's what matters most.

As time passed, I also learned to give myself permission to move forward. About nine months after Oliver's death, my family decided to bring a new dog, Bertie, into our lives. At first, I struggled with the idea of getting another dog, feeling like I was somehow replacing Oliver or betraying his memory. But eventually, I realized that Oliver had taught me how much love I had to give, and opening my heart to Bertie wasn't about replacing anyone—it was about continuing that love.

In the end, I've come to understand that grief and guilt are natural when we lose a pet, but they don't define the relationship we had with them. The love we share is what truly matters, and that love is what helps us move forward, even when it feels impossible at first.

Chapter 3:

Grief Isn't Linear—What to Expect

Grief is a deeply personal experience, one that doesn't follow any particular path or schedule. Unlike many aspects of life, it isn't something that can be neatly organized or checked off as complete. For each person, the journey of grieving is different, shaped by their emotions, memories, and the unique bond they shared with the one they've lost. And just when it seems like things have settled, grief can resurface unexpectedly, catching us off guard.

Although we often hear about stages like denial, anger, sadness, and acceptance, these are not steps that unfold in a straight line. Instead, they ebb and flow, sometimes overlapping or repeating in no predictable order. Understanding this helps us recognize that whatever we're feeling is part of the natural process, not something to be rushed or fixed. Some days may feel heavier than others, and certain moments may trigger deep feelings, even years later.

To give this perspective life, it can be helpful to hear from those who have walked this road before. Real stories from pet owners, for instance, offer glimpses into how grief has affected different people. Some may have found solace quickly, while others continue to feel waves of loss long after. There is no right or wrong way to grieve and no set timeline to follow. What matters is giving yourself the space to feel these emotions fully without expecting them to make sense or fade away quickly.

As time passes, grief does change. It may soften or shift, but it doesn't simply disappear. Learning to care for yourself during these moments of overwhelming emotion is essential. Whether it's through simple acts of kindness toward yourself, leaning on a support system, or finding ways to honor the loss, these are important steps in navigating this difficult process. Even after the intensity of the initial pain lessens, it's not unusual for a sudden memory, a familiar scent, or a special date to bring a fresh wave of sadness. Allowing yourself to experience these moments without judgment or pressure to move on can be one of the most important parts of healing.

Grief may not follow a predictable path, but in its unpredictability, there is a natural rhythm that, in time, will guide you through it.

The Stages of Grief

These stages—denial, anger, sadness (or depression), and acceptance—are often discussed to help people make sense of what they are feeling. However, it's important to know that grief doesn't follow a clear path. Instead, it is a personal and fluid process, meaning these stages can come and go, sometimes without warning, and often overlap (Holland, 2024).

Denial

When we experience loss, especially a profound one like the death of a loved one or the passing of a cherished pet, the first reaction many people have is **denial**. In this stage, it's as if your mind is trying to protect you from the full impact of the loss all at once. You might find yourself thinking, *This can't be happening*, or *This isn't real*. It's not uncommon, for instance, to still expect your loved one to walk through the door or to think you can call them, only to be jolted by the painful reality.

Denial helps create a buffer between you and the immediate emotional overload that often comes with grief. It gives you time—time to slowly begin processing what has happened. The feelings of disbelief allow your mind to absorb the reality of the situation gradually. As time goes on, though, this protective layer starts to lift, and other emotions, which may have been hidden beneath the surface, begin to rise.

Anger

Once the initial shock wears off, many people begin to experience **anger**. This can be one of the more surprising stages of grief because, often, you don't expect to feel angry after a loss. But anger is a natural response, and in many cases, it arises from the deep hurt and sense of injustice that comes with losing someone or something important to you. You might be angry at yourself, others, or even the situation itself.

For example, you may find yourself thinking, *Why didn't I do more?* or *Why did this happen to us?* In some cases, people may feel angry at the person they lost, even though they know it isn't rational. This anger can be directed at doctors, family members, or even the person or pet that has passed away, despite knowing, deep down, that they are not to blame. Anger is an outward expression of the intense pain and confusion swirling inside, and it's important to allow yourself to feel it without guilt. It's part of the healing process.

Sadness

As the anger begins to fade, it is often followed by **sadness** or **depression**. This stage of grief tends to be quieter but no less powerful. In fact, it is often during this phase that the full weight of the loss really begins to settle in. The sadness you feel may come in waves, sometimes overwhelming you and at other times receding into the background, only to return again unexpectedly.

You may find yourself crying without warning, feeling exhausted, or struggling to find joy in the things that once made you happy. The sadness can feel all-encompassing, almost like you're stuck in a fog, unsure how to move forward. It's not uncommon to want to withdraw from others during this time, preferring solitude to social interaction. This, too, is a normal response to grief. While it might feel isolating, it's important to remember that experiencing this depth of emotion is part of working through your loss.

Acceptance

After moving through the various stages of grief, some people eventually come to a place of **acceptance**. This stage doesn't mean that the pain of the loss is gone or that you have "moved on." Instead, acceptance is about finding a way to live with the loss. It's about acknowledging that life has changed, and while things will never be the same, you can still move forward.

In this stage, you might find that the sharp edges of grief have softened. You may still have moments of sadness, but they are less frequent and less overwhelming. Acceptance allows you to start thinking about the future again, not because you have forgotten your loved one, but because you are learning to carry their memory with you in a way that allows you to heal. You begin to rebuild, and with time, life becomes more manageable.

Emotions in the Grieving Process

The emotional experience of grief is far more complex than the stages alone suggest. In addition to denial, anger, sadness, and acceptance, there are often other feelings woven into the grieving process. **Guilt**, for example, is common. You may wonder if you could have done more or if there was something you missed. This feeling of "if only" can be especially strong when a decision is made about medical care or the timing of treatment. It's important to remind yourself that grief often brings a sense of helplessness, and no one can control every outcome.

Similarly, **loneliness** often accompanies grief, particularly when the person or pet lost plays a significant role in your daily life. This loneliness may not only be about missing the person or pet but also about feeling disconnected from the world around you. The routines you once shared with them may feel empty, and the loss can create a sense of isolation. You might find it difficult to re-engage with others, especially if they don't seem to understand the depth of your grief.

Alongside these emotions, some people may also experience **relief**—particularly in situations where the person or pet suffered from a prolonged illness. This relief does not lessen the grief, but it can be confusing, as it seems at odds with the sadness. It's okay to feel both at the same time.

Grief Is Not a Straight Line

One of the most important things to understand about grief is that it is not a linear process. You may find yourself revisiting certain stages—moving from sadness to anger, back to denial, and then to acceptance, only to feel the sadness return. And that's perfectly normal. The experience of grief is deeply personal, and there is no "right" way to go through it.

You might also find that certain triggers, like anniversaries or special memories, bring back emotions you thought had passed. These feelings are part of your ongoing relationship with the person or pet you lost, and while they may never fully go away, they will likely become easier to carry with time.

How Grief Changes Over Time and Why It's Important to Let It Unfold Naturally

These real-life stories help show that grief, especially after losing a pet, doesn't just go away after a set period of time. It changes, it evolves, but it remains a part of daily life. At first, the grief can feel like an unbearable weight, something that consumes every part of your life. Many people, like Quinn, describe those early days of grief as being filled with a sense of disbelief. Quinn remembers how she kept hearing her dog Ruby's nails on the floor, thinking that Ruby was still there when, in reality, she was gone. It was almost as if Quinn's mind couldn't fully accept the loss, and this was a natural part of the grieving process.

Over time, the sharpness of the pain may begin to soften. The loss doesn't disappear, but it becomes more bearable. People like Elizabeth learn to carry the grief with them in smaller, more manageable ways, like marking special days to honor their pets' memory or keeping mementos close by. The important thing to remember is that grief doesn't follow a strict timeline, and it's crucial to let it unfold naturally. Trying to rush through it or push the pain away can make the healing process even harder. Grief, when allowed to take its course, will shift and change over time, though the love for a lost pet never fades.

Common Emotions in the Grieving Process

As these stories have shown, there is a wide range of emotions that accompany the grieving process. **Guilt** is a common feeling for many people, especially if they have to make the heartbreaking decision to put their pet to sleep. Anonymous, who lost their dog after a tragic accident, struggled with guilt for months afterward. They even reached out to a pet psychic for comfort, which helped them see their dog's passing in a new light. They learned that their dog felt like he had died a hero's death, which gave Anonymous peace and helped them let go of some of the guilt.

Loneliness is another emotion that many people experience after losing a pet. Trevor and his wife, for example, felt a profound sense of emptiness in their home without Penny. Pets often become such a significant part of daily life that their absence can make the world feel a little quieter, a little less full. This loneliness can be especially difficult to cope with, particularly when your pet is your main companion.

Finally, **anger** and **frustration** are also common emotions in grief. Danielle, who lost her cat while pregnant, shared how angry she felt—not just at the situation but at the timing. She felt robbed of future moments with her cat, and that sense of injustice can be a powerful part of the grieving process.

Tips for Self-Care When Grief Feels Overwhelming

When grief becomes too much, it's important to take care of yourself, both physically and emotionally. Here are a few tips that may help during those difficult moments:

Give Yourself Permission to Grieve

Natasha, who lost her cat, Abby, found that a weighted stuffed animal helped her cope with the nights when she couldn't sleep. Having something to hold on to gave her comfort. It's important to remember that it's okay to grieve in whatever way feels right to you—there's no "right" or "wrong" way to mourn a pet.

Seek Support From Others

Whether it's friends, family, or even professional counselors, sharing your feelings can help lighten the emotional burden. Jessica found comfort by speaking to Bentley's gravestone and talking to others who had experienced similar losses. Grief doesn't have to be faced alone.

Create a Memorial

Doing something to honor your pet's memory can be a powerful way to keep their spirit close. Elizabeth, for example, keeps flowers by her dog's ashes every month. Small rituals like this can provide a sense of connection and help you process the grief.

Be Kind to Yourself

Grieving takes time, and it can be exhausting. It's important to take care of your body as well as your emotions. Make sure you're eating, sleeping, and giving yourself time to heal, as Trevor and his wife did after Penny's passing. Self-care is essential when dealing with weight loss.

Handling Unexpected Waves of Sadness

Even long after a pet has passed, it's not uncommon for waves of sadness to hit out of nowhere. These moments can be triggered by anything—a familiar smell, a particular time of day, or a favorite place. Christina, for example, still finds herself overwhelmed by emotion when she thinks of Tiger, even though it's been years since her passing. These moments don't mean you're not healing; they are just part of carrying the love and memories of your pet with you.

These moments can help to remind yourself that grief is not a straight line. Allow yourself to feel those emotions fully. Natasha found that her weighted stuffed animal brought her comfort during these waves of sadness, and other pet owners might find comfort in similar small acts of self-care. Whether it's sitting quietly with your memories, talking to a friend, or spending time in nature, it's important to let yourself grieve, even long after the initial loss.

Chapter 4:

Memorializing Your Pet and Creating Lasting Tributes

Losing a beloved pet can be an incredibly difficult experience, one that touches us deeply and often lingers long after they're gone. Pets quickly become part of our families. They are there through the highs and lows of life, offering us companionship, unconditional love, and endless joy. And when they are no longer with us, it's natural to feel an emptiness that's hard to describe. It can feel like we've lost a part of ourselves.

In these moments of loss, honoring your pet's memory can be a powerful way to begin the healing process. By memorializing your pet, you are not only holding on to the special bond you shared, but you are also giving yourself the space to reflect on the joy and love they brought into your life. And what's important to remember is that there are so many different ways to keep their spirit alive. It doesn't have to be something grand or formal, but something that feels right for you and your family.

For many, simple gestures can bring a lot of comfort. Writing a letter to your pet, for example, can be a very personal way of expressing all the things that you maybe didn't get the chance to say. It can give you a sense of closeness, even though they are no longer by your side. Some people might find comfort in creating a photo album, one that captures all of the special moments you shared with your pet—from their playful antics to the quiet times when they just sat beside you. For others, creating a lasting tribute like planting a tree or dedicating a small garden to your pet's memory can be a beautiful way to honor them. Over time, as the tree grows or the flowers bloom, it becomes a living reminder of the bond you shared. Every time you visit that space, you can feel a sense of connection to your pet, and that can be comforting, especially on those harder days when you miss them a little more than usual.

Memorial ceremonies can also offer a sense of closure. These ceremonies don't have to be large or formal; they can be as simple as gathering at home with family and close friends to share memories and say goodbye. Involving children in these ceremonies can be especially helpful for them, as it gives them a chance to process their own feelings of loss. It can also be a way to help them learn how to honor and remember someone they love in a meaningful way.

If you're someone who enjoys hands-on projects, creating a memory box or a scrapbook can be a deeply personal and healing way to remember your pet. Filling a memory box with things that remind you of your pet—their collar, a favorite toy, or even a handwritten note about your favorite memory with them—can be a comforting way to keep their spirit close. A scrapbook with photos, notes, and little mementos can become a keepsake that you can revisit whenever you want to feel connected to your pet.

Why Memorializing Your Pet Can Help With the Grieving Process

Losing a pet is one of the most heartbreaking experiences we can go through. When they pass away, it often leaves an emptiness that is difficult to fill. While the pain of their loss can be overwhelming, memorializing your pet can actually be an important step in helping you through the grieving process. It gives you a way to honor their memory and the time you spent together, allowing you to hold on to the love and joy they brought into your life.

When a pet dies, the grief can feel just as intense as when we lose a person close to us. For many people, their pet was a constant presence in their daily routine, offering comfort, loyalty, and often a sense of purpose. Suddenly, when they are gone, it's like a part of your world is missing. This emptiness can be hard to manage, and it's completely natural to feel lost without them. Memorializing your pet in whatever way feels right to you can provide a tangible way to process these feelings and keep their memory alive in a meaningful way.

One of the key reasons memorializing a pet helps with grieving is that it allows you to focus on the happy memories rather than just the sadness of their passing. It gives you an opportunity to reflect on all the moments of joy, love, and laughter your pet brought into your life. This shift in focus—from loss to remembrance—can be very healing. For example, you might find that creating a photo album or planting a tree in their memory brings back those cherished memories that remind you why your pet was so special.

Another reason memorializing your pet is helpful is because it provides a sense of closure. Grief often leaves us feeling as though there is unfinished business, as if we haven't properly said goodbye. By creating a lasting tribute, you give yourself a way to honor your pet's life in a concrete, physical way. Whether it's through a memorial service, a keepsake, or even just a small corner in your home dedicated to your pet's memory, having this place or item to turn to when you're missing them can be incredibly comforting. It serves as a reminder that while they are no longer physically with you, their memory will always have a special place in your heart.

And let's not forget that memorializing your pet can also open up a space for you to share your grief with others. The loss of a pet can sometimes feel isolating, as not everyone understands the deep bond you may have had. But through memorials, you can invite others to acknowledge and support you in your grief. This sense of community can bring a much-needed sense of comfort and validation during such a difficult time.

Creative Ways to Memorialize Your Pet

There are countless ways to memorialize a pet, and what's important is finding an option that feels personal and meaningful to you. Here are some creative ways that you might consider as you honor your pet's life:

Writing Letters to Your Pet

One of the simplest yet most heartfelt ways to remember your pet is by writing them a letter. It may feel a bit unusual at first, but writing down your thoughts, emotions, and memories can be an incredibly healing experience. You could write about how much you miss them, talk about your favorite memories, or even express the gratitude you feel for the time you had together. Sometimes, when words are difficult to speak, writing them down offers a release. It allows you to capture the emotions swirling inside and put them into words, which can be a powerful way to process your grief.

What's wonderful about writing letters is that you can return to this activity whenever you feel the need. You might write one letter right after your pet's passing, and later, as time passes, you might find yourself wanting to write more—maybe on their birthday or during moments when you miss them the most. These letters can be saved in a journal or notebook that becomes a cherished keepsake of your relationship with your pet. Whenever you want to feel close to them, you can open the journal and revisit those moments, giving you a space to reflect on your love for them.

Creating a Photo Album or Memory Box

Another beautiful way to memorialize your pet is by creating a photo album or memory box. This can be a simple but touching project that allows you to collect and preserve some of the most meaningful memories you shared with your pet. As you sift through old photographs, you may find yourself smiling as you remember all the moments of joy they brought into your life. You can arrange the photos in a special album, adding captions or little notes that capture the stories behind each picture. Maybe it's a photo of the first day you brought them home or one of them lounging in their favorite spot in the house. Each photo holds a special memory that you'll want to keep close to your heart.

Alongside the photos, you can also add mementos—things like their collar, their favorite toy, or even a small lock of their fur. Placing these items in a memory box turns it into a tangible collection of memories, something you can turn to whenever you're missing them. The act of gathering these items can also help you reflect on the happiness they brought into your life and the bond you shared.

This memory box or album doesn't have to be large or elaborate. Even a small, simple collection can hold deep meaning, as each item represents a connection to your pet. Whenever you're feeling particularly sad, having this physical reminder of your time together can provide a sense of comfort and help you feel closer to them, even after they've passed.

Planting a Tree or Creating a Memorial Garden

For those who find peace in nature, planting a tree or creating a memorial garden in honor of your pet can be a truly special way to remember them. If your pet loved spending time outdoors, playing in the yard, or basking in the sun, a tree or garden can be a living tribute that continues to grow and thrive in their memory. Each time you look at the tree or visit the garden, it will serve as a reminder of your pet's lasting presence in your life.

You could plant a tree in a spot that your pet loves to explore or create a small garden with flowers and plants that remind you of them. For instance, if your dog loves to chase butterflies, you might plant butterfly-attracting flowers. If your cat enjoys sitting in the sunlight, you could design the garden around their favorite sunlit spot. Over time, as the plants grow and bloom, they become a symbol of the life and love that continues on, even after your pet has passed.

To add a more personal touch, you might also consider placing a small memorial stone or plaque in the garden with your pet's name engraved on it. This gives you a specific place to visit and reflect on whenever you're feeling connected to your pet's memory. Some people even create little outdoor spaces with benches where they can sit and spend time thinking about their pets while surrounded by the beauty of nature.

Custom Art and Memorial Jewelry

For those who want something a bit more creative or artistic, custom portraits and memorial jewelry can be wonderful ways to honor your pet's memory. Many artists specialize in pet portraits, and having a custom painting or drawing made can be a lasting tribute to your furry friend. These portraits can capture your pet's unique personality, and hanging the artwork in your home will remind you daily of the love you shared.

If you're looking for something more personal, memorial jewelry is another option. Some people choose to have their pet's paw print or nose print engraved into a piece of jewelry, such as a necklace, ring, or bracelet. This way, you can carry a small part of your pet with you wherever you go, keeping them close to your heart. Others may choose to incorporate a small portion of their pet's ashes into a pendant or charm, allowing for a more physical connection to their memory.

Custom art and jewelry provide a heartfelt way to honor your pet's memory, serving as meaningful keepsakes that celebrate the bond you shared.

Holding a Memorial Service

For many, holding a memorial service for a beloved pet can offer a meaningful way to say goodbye and celebrate their life. You can gather with close friends and family, perhaps in your home or garden, and share stories and memories or even light candles in their honor. The act of coming together to remember your pet creates a shared experience of grief, allowing everyone to celebrate the joy and companionship your pet brought into your lives.

This doesn't have to be a formal or elaborate event. It can be as simple as inviting a few loved ones over to sit and talk about your pet, sharing photos, and reminiscing about the moments that made them special. Memorial services can help bring a sense of closure, giving you and those who loved your pet a chance to say goodbye in a way that honors their memory.

Ideas for Family and Community Involvement in Remembering Your Pet

Pets often touch the lives of more than just the person who feeds them or takes them for walks. They become an important part of family gatherings, evening routines, and even neighborhood strolls. So, when it comes to remembering them, it makes sense to involve those who shared those moments of love and joy with your pet.

Family Involvement

One of the most significant ways to bring the family together is to give everyone a chance to express their own memories of the pet. Sitting down as a family and talking about all the little moments that made your pet special can be incredibly healing. You could set aside an evening where everyone gathers in the living room, and each person takes a turn sharing their favorite story or moment. Maybe your child remembers how your dog always jumped up excitedly whenever they got home from school, or maybe your partner recalls the time your cat snuggled up during a cold winter night. These memories not only keep your pet's spirit alive, but they also help each family member feel connected to one another through shared grief.

Involving children in this process is especially important. Young children may not fully understand what has happened, and giving them an opportunity to talk about their feelings can help them process the loss. You might ask them to draw a picture of their favorite memory with your pet or even write a little letter expressing how much they miss their furry friend. This helps them feel included and gives them a way to express emotions they may not know how to put into words.

For families with more than one child, you could turn this into a family project by creating a memory box together. Each person can contribute something—a toy, a collar, a photo, or even a written note—to be placed inside the box. Then, whenever someone wants to feel close to the pet, they can open the box and relive those happy memories together.

Simple At-Home Ceremonies

One idea for a simple ceremony is to hold it in a special spot in your home or garden. You might gather everyone together in the backyard, especially if your pet loved to spend time outdoors or choose a cozy spot inside the house where your pet often slept or played. During the ceremony, you can light candles in your pet's memory, share stories, or even play a favorite song that reminds you of your time together.

If you have young children, you could involve them by letting them place their drawings or notes for the pet in a special place during the ceremony. For example, if you've set up a small memorial area with a framed picture of your pet or a few of their belongings, children could place their contributions there as part of the ritual. This makes the ceremony more interactive and gives children a way to participate in a way that feels meaningful to them.

You can also personalize the ceremony by reading a poem or a special letter you've written to your pet. It could be a letter expressing your love for them, thanking them for all the joy they brought into your life, or simply saying goodbye. Some people also find comfort in reciting a favorite poem that captures the depth of their bond with their pet. This quiet reflection can bring a sense of peace and closure.

DIY Projects to Honor Your Pet

In addition to memorial ceremonies, creating DIY projects that honor your pet can be a hands-on way for the whole family to engage with the grieving process. These projects allow you to personalize your tribute and create lasting keepsakes that you can cherish for years to come.

Scrapbooks

Another creative project is making a scrapbook dedicated to your pet. You can gather all of your favorite photos, written memories, and even small mementos to include in the book. You could organize the scrapbook in a way that tells the story of your pet's life, from when you first brought them home to their last days with you.

Scrapbooks allow for a lot of creative freedom, as you can decorate the pages with stickers, captions, and drawings. This project can be particularly therapeutic, as you're not only remembering your pet but also actively creating something beautiful that honors their memory.

DIY Paw Prints

If you still have access to your pet's paw print or want to create a keepsake from a print you've already made, turning that into a DIY project can be another touching way to remember them. You can use clay or plaster to create a paw print mold, and once it's dried, you can paint it or write your pet's name on it. These keepsakes can be framed or displayed in your home, providing a permanent and personal reminder of your pet's presence.

Chapter 5:

The Practical Aftermath—What to Do After Your Pet Passes

Losing a pet is one of the hardest things a person can go through. The grief that follows can feel overwhelming, and during such a time, it's easy to feel lost in your emotions. However, along with the sadness, there are also practical things that need to be handled. These steps, while necessary, can often seem impossible to face when you're already struggling to cope with the loss itself. But knowing what to do and when to do it can bring a small sense of clarity during a confusing and emotional time.

It's normal for many people to feel unsure of what comes next when a pet passes. You may find yourself thinking about questions you hadn't considered before, such as whether you should cremate or bury your pet or whether it's important to have a memorial service to honor their memory. All of these decisions can feel overwhelming, especially when your heart is heavy with grief.

On top of these personal decisions, there are also practical steps that have to be taken. These might include contacting your vet to ensure that all procedures are followed, as there may be legal considerations involved. Some people may not realize that things like vet certificates or legal steps could be required, depending on where you live, and understanding these requirements ahead of time can help avoid any surprises later on. It's these small but essential tasks that can make a difficult situation more manageable, though they may seem like a lot to handle at the moment.

Finding the right way to discuss the loss and what happens next can bring everyone closer together and provide a sense of shared comfort.

How to Handle the Logistics After a Pet Passes

When your beloved pet passes away, it can feel like the world has stopped for a moment, and it's completely natural to feel overwhelmed. Losing a pet is an emotional experience, but there are important steps you need to take in the hours immediately following their death. Handling the logistics thoughtfully can help ensure that your pet's final moments are treated with the respect and care they deserve. Let's talk about the steps to follow after your pet passes, including how to make decisions about cremation, burial, or memorial services.

Immediate Steps to Take After Your Pet Passes

Once you realize that your pet has passed, it's important to pause for a moment and let the reality of the situation settle in. There is no need to rush through this process. It's perfectly okay to spend a little time with your pet. Many people find comfort in sitting with their pets, holding them, or just quietly reflecting on their life. These moments can provide an opportunity for closure before moving on to the necessary next steps.

Confirming the Passing

If your pet passed away at home, you might feel uncertain about whether they have truly passed. You can gently check for any signs of breathing or feel for a heartbeat by placing your hand over their chest. If you are still unsure, it's always okay to call your veterinarian. They can either guide you over the phone or arrange for you to bring your pet in for confirmation. This step is essential, especially if the passing occurred at home without veterinary supervision (Buzby, 2020).

Contacting Your Veterinarian

After you've taken some time to process the loss, the next practical step is to contact your veterinarian. Most veterinary offices are equipped to help guide you through what happens next. They can offer advice on aftercare options, such as cremation or burial, and may even help arrange these services for you. Even if your pet passes away at home, many veterinarians work closely with local crematories or pet cemeteries and can assist in transporting your pet there if needed.

Transporting Your Pet

If your veterinarian cannot come to your home to collect your pet's body, or if you prefer to handle this yourself, you will need to prepare to transport your pet. This can be an emotional step, but with a bit of preparation, it can be done smoothly. You may want to wrap your pet in a soft blanket and gently place them in a suitable container or box for transport. If this feels too overwhelming, there are also specialized services that can come to your home to help you with the process.

Deciding on Aftercare Options

One of the most important decisions you will need to make after your pet's passing is what to do with their body. The two primary options for aftercare are burial or cremation. Each option carries its own considerations, so it's important to reflect on what feels right for you and your family.

Burial Options

For many pet owners, the idea of burying their pet at home offers a sense of comfort. It allows you to keep your pet close, and you can visit the resting place whenever you feel the need to. If you choose this option, you will need to check local regulations first. Some areas permit pet burials on private property, while others may have restrictions. If home burial is allowed, you will need to dig a grave that is at least 4 feet 1.2 inches deep to prevent other animals from disturbing the site. Wrapping your pet in biodegradable material, like a blanket, is recommended. Many people also choose to mark the grave with a special plant, stone, or small memorial plaque.

If home burial is not an option, you might consider a pet cemetery. Pet cemeteries offer a dignified and serene space where your pet can rest, and the upkeep is handled by the cemetery staff. This means you don't have to worry about maintenance, but it also means you might need to travel to visit the site. There are costs involved, including the plot, burial service, and any ongoing maintenance fees, but for many, the peace of mind this option provides makes it worthwhile.

Cremation Options

Cremation is another common choice, offering flexibility in how you memorialize your pet. There are two main types of cremation to consider: communal and individual cremation.

Communal Cremation

In communal cremation, multiple pets are cremated together, and the ashes are not returned to the owner. This is generally a more affordable option for those who do not feel the need to keep their pet's ashes. After the cremation, the ashes are often scattered in a shared memorial garden at the crematory, which can be a comforting thought for some families. It's important to confirm with the crematory how the ashes will be handled, as each facility may have different practices.

Individual Cremation

For those who wish to keep their pet's ashes, individual cremation is the best option. In this process, your pet is cremated alone, and their ashes are returned to you. Many people find comfort in having their pet's ashes in a special urn or keepsake that can be placed in their home. Depending on the crematory, you may also have the option to spend time with your pet before the cremation or even witness the process, which can provide an additional sense of closure.

Tips for Making Decisions Calmly

Making decisions after the loss of a pet is incredibly difficult, especially when you're dealing with so many emotions. It's a time when you might feel overwhelmed, and that's perfectly normal. But even during such emotional times, it's important to approach the choices ahead calmly and thoughtfully. In the days following your pet's passing, it's easy to feel pressured to make quick decisions, but rushing is often unnecessary. Taking a moment to gather your thoughts and breathe deeply can make all the difference in ensuring that you're making choices you'll feel at peace with later on.

Give Yourself Permission to Pause

It's very natural to feel like you need to act immediately after your pet passes, but most of the time, there is no need to rush. You don't have to decide on burial or cremation right away, nor do you have to make plans for memorials immediately. Allow yourself some time to sit with your grief before diving into these decisions. A few hours or even a day of rest can help you approach things with a clearer mind. In fact, many veterinarians and aftercare services understand that grieving pet owners may need time, and they are often very accommodating.

Ask for Help From Trusted Friends or Family

Sometimes, just talking things through with a close friend or family member can help ease the burden of decision-making. If you're feeling unsure about what to do next, don't hesitate to reach out. They may have a perspective you hadn't considered, or they can simply listen as you talk through your thoughts. Even though the final decision will be yours, having someone by your side to share ideas or offer a calming presence can make the process a little less daunting.

Break Down the Decisions Into Smaller, Manageable Steps

When you're in the middle of an emotional situation, making decisions all at once can feel overwhelming. Instead of thinking about everything that needs to be done, it might help to break it down into smaller steps. For example, start by deciding whether you prefer cremation or burial. Once that's settled, move on to the details of how you want to carry out that option, such as choosing a crematorium or considering a pet cemetery. By focusing on one step at a time, each decision becomes less overwhelming.

Take Time to Reflect on What Feels Right for You

When making these decisions, it's important to listen to what feels right for you personally. There are no wrong choices here—whether you choose cremation, a home burial, or a pet cemetery, what matters most is that the option you select brings you peace. Sometimes, people feel pressured by what others might think they should do, but this is about honoring your pet in the way that feels most meaningful to you. Taking a little time to reflect on what would help you say goodbye can make the decision easier.

Write Down Your Options

When emotions are running high, it's easy to forget or lose track of important details. Writing down your thoughts can help bring clarity and organize the decisions in front of you. Whether you're exploring cremation services or thinking about different ways to memorialize your pet, putting everything on paper (or in a notes app) allows you to see your options clearly. It also gives you something to refer back to later, especially if you're feeling uncertain.

Resources for Finding Support

Navigating grief can feel isolating, but the good news is that you don't have to go through it alone. There are numerous resources designed to support people going through the loss of a pet, from grief hotlines to online communities where you can connect with others who are experiencing the same pain. Knowing where to turn for support can make all the difference.

Grief Hotlines

If you need someone to talk to in those difficult moments, a pet loss hotline can be an excellent resource. For instance, the Cornell Pet Loss Support Hotline is available a few evenings a week, and it's staffed by trained veterinary students who are experienced in handling calls about pet loss. They offer a compassionate ear and can help you process the emotions you're feeling. Many other hotlines provide similar services, offering a safe space to talk about your loss (Cummings School of Veterinary Medicine, n.d.).

Online Support Groups

The internet provides a wealth of support options that can connect you with people who truly understand the depth of your loss. Online support groups are often made up of individuals who are experiencing or have experienced similar situations, and sharing your feelings with others who truly understand can bring significant comfort. The Association for Pet Loss and Bereavement provides organized chat rooms and video support groups, offering a space to connect with others and receive emotional support. There are also numerous informal groups on social media, like Facebook, where people gather to share stories, offer advice, and simply support one another (Smith et al., 2024).

In-Person Support Groups

For those who prefer face-to-face interactions, local support groups can offer a comforting space to share your grief. Many veterinary schools and clinics, like the Michigan State University Veterinary Medical Center, host pet loss support meetings. These meetings provide a chance to gather with others who are experiencing similar emotions and share your stories. Sometimes, just knowing you're not alone in your grief can make it a little more bearable (Arora et al., 2020).

Grief Counseling

If you're finding it difficult to cope with the loss on your own, professional grief counseling may be the support you need. Therapists who specialize in grief, particularly pet loss, can help guide you through this emotional time with coping strategies and emotional tools to manage the pain. Services like Lap of Love even offer individual counseling sessions, which can be incredibly helpful for those who feel overwhelmed by their grief. Don't hesitate to reach out to a grief counselor if you need more support—there is no shame in asking for help.

Legal Considerations

While the emotional aspect of losing a pet is understandably the most pressing concern, there may also be some legal considerations depending on how you choose to handle your pet's remains. These considerations are usually straightforward but important to keep in mind as you make decisions.

Veterinary Assistance With Aftercare

If your pet passed away under the care of a veterinarian, they will usually handle some of the initial steps for you, such as confirming the death and providing aftercare options. Many veterinary offices are already connected with local crematoriums or pet cemeteries, so they can guide you through the process, help arrange transportation, or handle other necessary steps. This can ease some of the burden during a very difficult time.

Home Burial Regulations

For those who wish to bury their pet at home, it's important to first check your local regulations. In some areas, home burial is perfectly legal, but there may be restrictions regarding burial depth, proximity to water sources, or whether or not you own the property. You can check with your local authorities or city office to make sure you are following the rules and that the burial is safe and legal. This can prevent any complications down the road (Kessler, 2021).

Environmental Guidelines for Cremation

Cremation, particularly communal cremation, generally does not come with extensive legal restrictions. However, if you plan to scatter your pet's ashes in a public space, like a park or beach, you might need to check with local authorities. Some areas have regulations regarding the scattering of ashes to ensure that the environment is not negatively impacted. Most crematoriums can also provide guidance on what's appropriate and legally permitted if you're unsure (Kessler, 2021).

Disposal of Euthanized Pet Remains

If your pet was euthanized, there may be special considerations when it comes to the disposal of their remains. The drugs used in euthanasia, such as pentobarbital, stay in the body after death. Because of this, home burial might not be advisable in some areas, as the drug could seep into water sources or affect the environment. You may need to check with your veterinarian or local government to ensure that the burial is safe and that there are no specific disposal requirements.

How to Talk to Children About What Happens Next

When it comes to children, their understanding of death and loss depends a lot on their age and developmental stage. Younger children may not fully grasp the concept of permanence, while older kids might already have some understanding but still need guidance on what happens next. Here's how to approach it in a thoughtful, supportive way:

Be Clear and Honest While Remaining Gentle

Children need clear explanations to help them understand what has happened. Instead of using phrases like "Fluffy went to sleep" or "Buddy ran away," which might confuse them or even make them anxious about sleeping or pets disappearing, it's best to use direct language. You could say something like, "Fluffy has died, and that means her body has stopped working, and she won't be coming back." This is hard to say, but it helps the child understand that their pet is no longer physically here without introducing more fear or misunderstanding into their lives.

You can gently explain that while the pet's body no longer works, their memory and the love they shared will always be with them. Something like, "Even though Buddy isn't here with us anymore, we'll always remember how much fun we had playing with him in the yard."

Encourage Questions and Be Ready to Answer

Children are naturally curious, and after hearing about their pet's death, they may have a lot of questions. They might ask things like, "Why did Fluffy die?" or "Where is Buddy now?" It's important to answer their questions honestly while keeping their age in mind. For younger children, you might say something simple like, "Fluffy's body was very tired, and it couldn't work anymore." For older kids, you can add more detail, explaining that sometimes pets get sick or grow old, and when that happens, their bodies can no longer keep up with all the things they used to do.

You may also encounter questions about what happens after death, like "Will I see Buddy again?" or "Is Fluffy in heaven?" These are deeply personal questions, and your answers will depend on your family's beliefs. If you're not sure how to answer, it's okay to say, "I don't know for sure, but I like to think Buddy is happy and at peace." This kind of openness allows the child to form their own understanding while still feeling comforted by your honesty.

Validate Their Feelings

One of the most important things you can do during this conversation is to let children know that their feelings are completely normal. They may feel sad, confused, or even angry. Reassuring them that these emotions are normal and valid is essential. You can say something like, "It's okay to feel sad and miss Fluffy. I miss her too." By acknowledging your own feelings, you show them that grief is something everyone experiences and it's not something they have to go through alone.

If your child feels angry or guilty, for example, if they're upset that they didn't spend more time with the pet, it's helpful to offer comfort. You might say, "Buddy loved you no matter what, and he knew how much you cared about him." This reassures them that their pet feels loved, even if they have regrets.

Involve Them in the Aftercare Process

Giving children a way to say goodbye or remember their pets can be very helpful for their emotional healing. You might involve them in simple tasks like choosing a spot for a burial, drawing a picture, writing a goodbye letter, or picking out a keepsake if you choose cremation. You could ask, "Would you like to help plant some flowers in Buddy's favorite spot in the yard so we can always remember him when we look outside?" These small acts allow children to express their love and grief in a tangible way.

Offer Reassurance for the Future

Sometimes, a child's grief might lead them to worry about other pets or loved ones. They might ask, "Will our other pets die too?" or "Will you die?" These are difficult questions, but it's important to offer reassurance without making promises that can't be kept. You could say, "Right now, our other pets are healthy, and we're taking good care of them. They'll be with us for a long time." Or if they ask about you or other family members, you can explain, "We're doing our best to stay healthy, and we're going to be here to take care of you for a long time."

How to Talk to Loved Ones About What Happens Next

Talking to other adults or older children in the family about the next steps after a pet's passing also requires care, but these conversations will likely focus more on practical decisions, like aftercare or memorials, while still honoring the emotional connection everyone shared with the pet.

Acknowledge the Shared Grief

Start by acknowledging that the loss is hard for everyone. You might say, "I know we're all feeling this loss, and it's been tough without Buddy around." By recognizing everyone's emotions, you create space for an open conversation where your loved ones feel comfortable sharing their feelings, too.

Discuss the Next Steps Together

After acknowledging the emotional weight of the situation, it's time to discuss what happens next. Depending on your loved one's involvement with the pet, they might want to be part of the decision-making process regarding cremation, burial, or memorial services. You could say, "I was thinking about having Buddy cremated, but I'd like to hear what you think. Do you have any thoughts on what would feel right for us?"

Bringing everyone into the conversation gives them a sense of ownership and helps ensure that whatever decisions are made feel right to the whole family. It also helps ease any potential tension or misunderstandings by ensuring that everyone's voice is heard.

Create Opportunities for Remembrance

Similar to how children benefit from being involved in memorial activities, adults and older children may also appreciate creating a way to remember the pet together. You could suggest a gathering to share stories, look at photos, or talk about their favorite moments. You might say, "Would it be helpful if we all spent some time together sharing our favorite memories of Fluffy? I think it would be nice to remember the joy she brought us."

Some families choose to hold a small memorial, plant a tree, or create a photo album in honor of their pet. These activities help loved ones process their grief by transforming their memories into something lasting and positive.

Be Supportive of Everyone's Grieving Process

It's important to recognize that everyone grieves differently, and that's okay. Some people may want to talk about the pet constantly, while others may withdraw for a bit. Offer your support by saying, "I'm here if you want to talk, but I also understand if you need some space right now." This helps loved ones feel supported without pressuring them to grieve in a certain way.

Look Forward to Healing Together

Lastly, it's helpful to remind loved ones that healing takes time but that you'll get through it together. You might say, "This has been really hard, but we have each other, and we'll keep moving forward." By focusing on the strength of your relationships and shared support, you provide comfort during a time of loss.

Chapter 6:

The Guilt Around Euthanasia—

Releasing the Burden

Making the decision to let go of a beloved pet through euthanasia is often one of the most emotionally challenging experiences a pet owner can face. The thought of saying goodbye can bring about feelings of guilt, sadness, and uncertainty, especially when we are deeply attached to our furry companions. However, even though it is difficult, euthanasia can sometimes be the most compassionate choice when a pet is suffering and their quality of life has declined.

For many, this decision can feel incredibly heavy, like a burden that weighs on the heart. There are often doubts and inner conflicts, with questions like, *Am I doing the right thing?* or *Is it too soon?* swirling through the mind. These are natural thoughts because our love for our pets makes it hard to accept that letting them go could be the kindest thing we can do for them. But it's important to remember that euthanasia, when chosen to relieve a pet from pain or illness, is not about giving up. Instead, it's an act of mercy, a final gift of peace that we can offer to our cherished animal companions.

Many people who have gone through this process will tell you that the feelings of guilt and sorrow are normal, but there is comfort in knowing that their decision was made out of love and kindness. Hearing stories from others who have faced this same heart-wrenching choice can provide some relief. These shared experiences remind us that we are not alone in this journey. They also help show that, while the grief of losing a pet may be complex and long-lasting, there is a certain peace that comes with knowing that we helped ease their suffering.

It's also essential to lean on the expertise and support of your veterinarian during this time. Your vet can explain the options and walk you through the steps involved in euthanasia, ensuring that your pet is treated with dignity and care. Talking with them openly can help you feel more at ease with the decision, as they can offer valuable guidance based on their professional experience.

Saying goodbye to your pet is never easy, but finding ways to make the process meaningful—whether through a final moment of closeness or a special ritual—can help honor the bond you've shared. The grief that follows, although intense, is something you don't have to face alone. There are resources and support networks available to help you navigate these complex emotions and begin the process of healing.

Why Euthanasia Can Feel Like a Heavy Burden

One of the reasons this choice feels so burdensome is because of the deep responsibility it places on us. As pet owners, we want what's best for our furry friends, and sometimes it's hard to know if we're making the right decision. You might find yourself wondering if you should wait a little longer, hoping for a miraculous recovery or at least one more good day. Pets are incredibly resilient, and they often hide their pain well, so it's not always easy to see how much they are truly suffering. This uncertainty can make you question your choice, and with that comes guilt—guilt over whether there's something more you could do or if you're acting too soon.

The emotional attachment we feel for our pets makes this decision even harder. Watching them grow older, seeing their health decline, and knowing they are in pain can be incredibly heartbreaking. But letting them go feels almost impossible at times. You might even feel as though you are betraying your pet, especially when they still have moments of joy or energy. It's a delicate balance of emotions that can make the decision feel so much heavier. But it's important to remember that choosing euthanasia is often the most loving decision you can make when their quality of life is no longer what it should be.

It allows them to rest, free from pain, and that is the ultimate gift we can give them.

Despite how difficult it is, euthanasia is an act of love. It's a way to prevent prolonged suffering and offer a peaceful end when there are no other options to improve their quality of life. While it may feel like a heartbreaking choice, it's also a kind one and one that can bring your pet the peace they deserve.

Talking to Your Veterinarian About Euthanasia Options

Veterinarians have a wealth of experience in helping pet owners navigate this emotional time, and they can provide both guidance and support. It's not uncommon to feel lost when trying to figure out whether it's time, and that's where your vet can really help you.

When discussing euthanasia with your veterinarian, don't hesitate to ask all the questions that come to mind. You might want to know if your pet is in pain, how much time they may have left, or whether there are treatments that could improve their quality of life. It's natural to seek as much information as possible before making a decision, and your veterinarian is there to help you understand all the options available. They can explain what the euthanasia process looks like, and, more importantly, they can reassure you that it is a gentle and peaceful procedure.

Veterinarians will typically use a sedative first to ensure your pet is calm and relaxed. Once your pet is at ease, a painless injection is administered, and they drift off into a deep, peaceful sleep before passing away. Knowing how the process works can ease some of the anxiety you may feel as you realize that this is a peaceful way for your pet to leave this world.

You may also want to talk to your vet about the timing and location of the procedure. Some people prefer to say their goodbyes at the veterinary clinic, while others may want to have the procedure done at home, where their pet feels most comfortable. Your veterinarian can help you decide what is best for your situation and your pet's needs. These conversations can make a very difficult decision feel more manageable, as they allow you to plan in a way that is best for both you and your pet.

How to Say Goodbye During the Euthanasia Process in a Meaningful Way

When the time comes to say goodbye, it can be overwhelming to think about how to make those final moments as meaningful and comforting as possible. However, there are ways to create a peaceful and loving environment during the euthanasia process, which can help bring a sense of closure and peace to both you and your pet.

One of the most important decisions you'll make is whether or not to be present during the euthanasia. Many pet owners find comfort in being there with their pets, holding them close, and talking to them during their final moments. This can be a deeply meaningful way to say goodbye, offering your pet the reassurance of your presence, love, and care. You can whisper comforting words, stroke their fur, or simply sit with them, letting them know they are not alone. For many, being present is a way to give their pet the same love in death as they gave throughout life.

If the euthanasia takes place at home, you might want to create a calm and familiar setting for your pet. You could place their favorite blanket nearby, surround them with their favorite toys, or even have a special treat on hand. These small touches can help your pet feel secure and loved as they transition from this life. If you choose to have family or friends present, this can also provide a sense of togetherness, as you all share honoring the life of your beloved pet. Being together in this moment can create a sense of comfort and closure, allowing everyone to say goodbye and support one another through the loss.

The Decision-Making Process

The decision to euthanize a pet is never straightforward, but one way to approach it is by considering your pet's overall quality of life. Many pet owners begin by reflecting on whether their pets are still able to enjoy the things that once made them happy. Are they still interested in food? Are they able to move comfortably? Are they still engaged with their surroundings, or do they seem withdrawn and distant? Answering these questions can help provide some clarity in an otherwise murky situation. Your veterinarian can also be an incredible guide in this process. They can help you assess your pet's health using quality-of-life scales, which are tools designed to measure your pet's well-being based on their pain levels, mobility, hunger, and overall happiness.

One helpful approach is to think about your pet's good days versus bad days. If the bad days are becoming more frequent and if their suffering seems to outweigh the joy they experience, it might be time to consider euthanasia. As painful as that is to think about, it can actually provide a sense of relief knowing that you are prioritizing their comfort and peace.

That being said, coming to terms with this decision takes time. It's okay to take as long as you need to process your feelings. Many pet owners find it helpful to talk things through with their veterinarian, who can explain what the process will look like and what to expect. It's also a good idea to lean on friends or family members who understand how deeply you love your pet. Sometimes, just having someone to talk to can make all the difference in feeling more at peace with the choice.

Stories From Others Who Faced This Decision and How They Found Comfort

Reading stories from other pet owners who have gone through the same experience can provide a sense of comfort and understanding.

For example, Melinda, the owner of a black Labrador named Belle, shared how she struggled with knowing when it was the right time to let her beloved dog go. Belle had been suffering from arthritis, and although Melinda tried everything she could—medications, physical therapy, and even special diets—Belle's condition continued to decline. Melinda's veterinarian helped guide her through the decision-making process by using a quality-of-life scale. Eventually, Melinda realized that as much as it hurt to say goodbye, it was time. Afterward, she felt a bittersweet sense of relief, knowing Belle was no longer in pain.

Another story that touches the heart is that of Anita Kelsey and her cat, Figgy. Anita spoke about how Figgy had battled kidney disease for years, and although she was still affectionate, her health had started to decline rapidly. Figgy began hiding away from her family, which is often a sign that cats are ready to let go. Anita made the difficult decision to have Figgy euthanized at home, where she could be surrounded by familiar sights and smells. Although it was incredibly hard to say goodbye, Anita found comfort in knowing that Figgy's passing was peaceful and free from fear. Her story reminds us that, while the decision to euthanize a pet is never easy, it can be a final act of kindness that spares them from unnecessary suffering.

Hearing these stories helps us remember that we are not alone in our grief and that other pet owners have faced the same heart-wrenching decision. Knowing that others have found peace and comfort after making this choice can be reassuring, especially in moments when we feel uncertain or overwhelmed.

After-Euthanasia Grief and How to Process Complex Emotions

After euthanasia, it's normal to feel a wide range of emotions—sadness, guilt, even relief. Grief is complex, and the loss of a pet can feel just as devastating as losing a close friend or family member. Our pets hold such a special place in our hearts, and the bond we share with them is unlike any other. When that bond is broken, the sadness can feel overwhelming.

One of the most common emotions pet owners feel after euthanasia is guilt. You may find yourself asking, *Did I make the right decision?* or *Could I have done more?* These thoughts are a natural part of the grieving process, but it's important to remember that you made your decision out of love. You did what was best for your pet, considering their comfort and well-being. Guilt often comes from a place of deep care, but over time, you can begin to recognize that your choice was a selfless act, one made to give your pet the peaceful end it deserved.

Grieving is different for everyone, and there's no right or wrong way to process these emotions. Some pet owners find comfort in creating a small memorial for their pet, like planting a tree or placing their ashes in a special urn. Others may find it helpful to talk to friends or family who understand their loss. Sharing stories about your pet, looking through photos, or simply talking about the joy they brought into your life can be healing. For some, seeking out support from a pet loss counselor or joining a grief group can provide additional help during this difficult time.

Another helpful way to process your emotions is by journaling or writing a letter to your pet. It might feel a little strange at first, but putting your feelings down on paper can help release some of the emotions you're holding on to. You can write about the love and joy your pet brought into your life and express any lingering feelings you may have. This private reflection can be a powerful way to say goodbye in your own words.

There is no timeline for healing. The pain of losing a pet may never completely disappear, but over time, the sharpness of that pain will soften. You'll start to remember the good times more clearly—the way they greeted you at the door, their favorite place to nap, or the little quirks that made them so special. These memories will bring comfort, and eventually, you'll find peace in knowing that you gave your pet a life full of love and a kind, compassionate farewell when they needed it most.

Grief is a journey, and it's okay to feel whatever you're feeling, whether it's sadness, anger, or even relief. Give yourself the time and space to heal, and lean on those who understand your pain. Just as you were there for your pet in life, you were there for them in their final moments, and that is something truly special.

Chapter 7:

Your Family (and Other Pets)

Through Grief

Losing a pet can be an incredibly difficult experience for everyone in the family. Pets, after all, often hold such a special place in our hearts, becoming cherished members of the household, so when they are no longer with us, it can create a deep sense of sadness. For children, this may even be their first time experiencing the loss of something they love, and they might not fully understand what has happened or how to express their feelings in words. At the same time, other pets in the home can also feel the loss, and sometimes they show signs of confusion or distress that we might not expect.

During this time, families are often faced with the challenge of trying to support one another while also dealing with their own emotions. It becomes important to create a space where everyone can take the time to process the loss together and feel comfortable openly sharing how they're feeling. Helping children to navigate through their emotions in an age-appropriate way can be especially important, as they need both understanding and comfort during such a difficult time. And, of course, it's just as important to recognize that the other pets in the home might be grieving, too. They may exhibit changes in their behavior, and as they adjust to the absence of their companion, they'll likely need extra care and attention to help them cope.

How to Help Children Understand and Process

Helping children understand and process the loss involves guiding them through difficult emotions while offering comfort and support, not just as individuals but as a whole family. Pets hold a special place in children's hearts; they are often playmates, sources of comfort, and loyal companions. So, when a pet passes away, the grief children feel can be profound. Understanding how to talk about this loss and support each other during such a time is crucial to healing as a family.

Grieving as a Family

The loss of a pet is a family experience, touching everyone in the household. The grief that follows can be complex because each family member has their own unique bond with the pet and may express their emotions differently. This is where family conversations and mutual support become invaluable. As a family, sitting down together and talking about the loss can provide a safe space for everyone to share their feelings.

For instance, you might find that some members of the family are eager to talk about their sadness, while others may prefer to remain quiet. It's important to recognize that these are both natural responses. You could start the conversation by simply acknowledging the loss: "I know we are all feeling sad because [pet's name] isn't with us anymore. It's okay to feel upset." This kind of opening invites everyone to express what they're going through in a way that feels comfortable to them.

Let your children know it's okay to cry, be angry, or even feel confused. Perhaps one child might be wondering why the pet had to die, while another could be feeling guilty for not spending more time with the pet before its death. In such cases, listen carefully and reassure them that these feelings are a normal part of grieving. You might say something like, "It's completely normal to feel sad or even mad right now. We all loved [pet's name], and it's okay to miss them."

When parents take the time to share their own feelings, it shows children that even adults struggle with loss and that it's okay to talk about these difficult emotions. You could gently share how you're feeling, perhaps saying, "I'm feeling sad too because I miss [pet's name], but talking about it helps me feel a little better." This lets your children know that they're not alone in their grief, and it provides a model for how to express emotions in a healthy way.

It's also important to continue checking in with each other over time. Grief doesn't end after one conversation. You might find that bringing up memories of the pet during family meals or even just before bed can offer comfort and encourage everyone to keep talking about how they're coping. For example, you could say, "Does anyone have a favorite memory of [pet's name] they'd like to share?" This can shift the focus toward the happy moments you all shared with the pet, helping to balance the sadness with positive reflections.

Explaining Death to Children in Age-Appropriate Ways

Explaining death to children is never easy, but it becomes more manageable when done in a way that suits their developmental stage. Each age group understands and processes death differently, so tailoring your explanation is essential to help them make sense of what has happened.

Toddlers and Preschoolers (Ages 2–5)

Children at this age have a limited understanding of death's permanence. They might not grasp that their pet isn't coming back, and they may repeatedly ask when they will see their pet again. It's important to use simple and clear language, avoiding confusing euphemisms. You could say, "When someone or a pet dies, their body stops working, and they don't feel pain or sadness anymore. We won't see [pet's name] again, but we can always remember the fun times we had." You might need to repeat this explanation multiple times, as young children often need reassurance and clarity. For instance, if they ask, "But where did [pet's name] go?" you can gently remind them,

"Remember, [pet's name]'s body stopped working, and that's why we won't see them again."

Children (Ages 6–10)

At this age, children begin to grasp that death is permanent, yet they may still hold misunderstandings or even feel somehow responsible. They may wonder if they did something wrong or if their pet could have lived longer if they had done things differently. It's important to reassure them by saying, "Our pet died because their body was very old or sick, and there was nothing we could do to stop it. It wasn't anyone's fault." This can help ease any guilt they might feel. Children at this stage are also more likely to ask detailed questions about what happens when a pet dies, and it's okay to provide simple, factual answers. For example, you can explain, "When a pet dies, their body stops working, and that means they don't eat, breathe, or feel anything anymore."

Preteens and Teens (Ages 11 and Up)

Older children and teenagers have a more mature understanding of death. They know it's final and irreversible, but that doesn't mean they don't have their own set of questions and emotional struggles. Teens may even experience complex feelings like anger, guilt, or deep sadness. They might also want to explore the topic of death in more depth, asking questions like "Why do pets have to die?" or "Why couldn't the vet save them?" Be open to these questions and answer them honestly. You might say, "Sometimes, even with all the care we give them, pets get too sick to get better, and dying is a part of life, as sad as it is." Encourage them to talk about their feelings in whatever way is most comfortable for them, whether through conversation, writing, or art. If they don't feel like talking right away, that's okay too—let them know you're there whenever they are ready.

Tips for Holding Family Conversations About the Loss

When the time comes to sit down as a family and talk about the pet's death, it's important to approach the conversation thoughtfully and with care. These conversations can be incredibly healing, but they also require sensitivity. Below are a few tips to help guide these discussions:

Create a Safe and Comfortable Environment

The setting of the conversation is important. Choose a time and place where everyone feels safe and comfortable to open up. This might be around the dinner table, during a quiet moment in the living room, or even outside during a family walk. The goal is to make sure there are no distractions and that everyone feels like they have the time and space to speak if they want to.

Start the Conversation Gently

You don't need to dive straight into deep emotions right away. You can ease into the conversation by acknowledging the loss and allowing space for everyone to share their initial thoughts. You could say, "I know we're all feeling sad because we loved [pet's name] so much. How are you all feeling right now?" This invites everyone to share at their own pace, whether they are ready to talk about their feelings or just need a moment to process them.

Use Clear and Simple Language

Avoid using vague or abstract terms that might confuse children, especially younger ones. Phrases like "passed away" or "went to sleep" might sound comforting to adults, but they can confuse children, who may take them literally. Instead, say things like, "Our pet died because their body wasn't working anymore, and that means we won't see them again." This clear, honest language helps children understand the situation without misunderstandings.

Encourage the Sharing of Memories

Talking about the happy moments you shared with your pet can be a great way to celebrate their life and make the conversation feel less heavy. You could ask, "What's one of your favorite memories with [pet's name]?" or "What funny thing did [pet's name] do that made you laugh the most?" This allows everyone to focus on the positive aspects of their relationship with the pet, which can bring some light to the grief.

Be Open to Different Reactions

Remember, everyone grieves in their own way. Some children might cry, others might not say much at all, and some might seem fine one day and upset the next. Be patient and understanding of these different reactions. Let them know that whatever they're feeling is okay. You might say, "It's okay if you don't feel like talking about [pet's name] right now, and it's also okay if you want to talk about them later."

Offer Involvement in Farewell Rituals

Allow children to be involved in any farewell or memorial rituals, but don't force them if they aren't ready. You could ask, "Would you like to help plan a special way to say goodbye to [pet's name]?" This could include a small ceremony, making a scrapbook, or writing a letter to the pet. Involving them in these rituals can give them a sense of closure and a way to process their grief.

Recognizing Grief in Other Pets

When a pet passes away, the grief felt within a family is often shared, not only among the humans but also with the other pets who were close to the one who has passed. Pets can form incredibly strong bonds with one another, just as they do with the people around them, and the absence of their companion can leave them feeling confused, anxious, and even distressed. Recognizing the signs of grief in surviving pets is essential, as they, too, need help to navigate the emotional void left behind. While they may not understand the concept of death in the way humans do, the change in their environment and the absence of their companion is something they will certainly feel. It's important to know how to support your surviving pet through this difficult transition.

Recognizing Grief in Other Pets

When one pet in a household dies, the remaining pets often notice the sudden absence of their friend. Pets rely heavily on routine and familiar relationships, so when a key part of their daily life is missing, they can become unsettled. Dogs, for example, may look for their lost companion around the house, searching in places where they used to play or sleep together. Similarly, cats, who might have shared a space or routine with the deceased pet, may exhibit behaviors like pacing or meowing in a more distressed tone. These behaviors are clear indicators that the surviving pet is not only aware of the loss but is also struggling to adjust to the change.

One of the most heartbreaking things you might notice is your pet looking around for their lost friend. They might walk to the spot where their companion used to sleep or sit by the door, waiting for them to return. They might sniff around more than usual or even paw at areas they associate with their friend. These behaviors, while sad to witness, are their way of processing the loss and trying to understand why things have changed. During this time, it's helpful to offer extra comfort and reassurance. Your pet may not understand what has happened, but they do know that something is different.

To support a grieving pet, it's important to maintain as much normalcy as possible. Pets thrive on routine, and the sudden absence of a companion can already be quite disruptive. By keeping feeding times, walks, and other daily activities consistent, you provide a sense of stability that can help them feel more secure. Routine gives them something predictable to hold on to in the midst of change. For example, if your dog is used to a morning walk with their lost companion, continue the walk, even if it's just the two of you. The familiar activity can provide some comfort.

Behavioral Changes in Other Pets After a Loss, and How to Ease Their Anxiety

When a pet is grieving, the emotional toll often manifests through noticeable changes in behavior. Much like people, animals can respond to loss in different ways, and their reactions can vary depending on their personality and the bond they share with the lost pet. Below are some common behavioral changes that grieving pets may exhibit, along with strategies to help ease their anxiety during this difficult time.

Change in Appetite

One of the more common signs of grief in pets is a sudden change in appetite. Some animals may lose interest in food altogether, while others might eat more than usual as a form of self-comfort. For example, a dog that used to eagerly share mealtime with its companion may now seem disinterested, leaving food in its bowl or refusing to eat. Cats, too, may show signs of disinterest, or they might meow for food but then leave it untouched. It's important to keep an eye on these eating habits because prolonged refusal to eat can lead to health complications. You might need to tempt them with favorite treats or hand-feed them if necessary. However, if their appetite doesn't return after a few days, it's wise to consult with a veterinarian to rule out any other health concerns that could be contributing to the change.

Increased Vocalization

Pets, particularly dogs and cats, might become more vocal when they are grieving. They may bark, howl, or meow more often, especially if they used to communicate with their lost companion. This increased vocalization is often a sign of distress or an attempt to call out for their friend. For instance, you might notice your dog standing by a window and barking more than usual or your cat meowing in a way that sounds more forlorn than before. These sounds can be their way of expressing confusion and sorrow. While it's difficult to hear, it's important to remain calm and offer them gentle comfort. Talking to them in soothing tones and spending extra time with them can help ease their distress.

Changes in Sleep Patterns

Just like people, pets may also experience disruptions in their sleep patterns after losing a companion. Some animals may sleep more than usual, possibly as a way to cope with their emotions, while others may have trouble settling down. You might find that your dog or cat, who was used to sleeping next to their companion, now struggles to rest or moves around the house at night, searching for a familiar presence that's no longer there. To help ease this, you could create a comforting space for them to sleep. Using blankets or items that carry the scent of the lost pet can sometimes offer them a sense of familiarity and comfort. If your pet is still restless, try spending extra time with them before bed, offering soothing words or gentle petting to help them feel more secure.

Clinginess or Withdrawal

The emotional bond between pets can be very strong, and when one pet dies, the remaining pet may either cling more to their human family members or withdraw altogether. Some pets become more affectionate, seeking constant attention and wanting to stay close to their humans as a way to feel safe. They may follow you around the house, sit by your side more frequently, or even try to sleep in the spot where their companion used to rest. On the other hand, some pets might do the opposite and become more distant. They may hide in quiet areas of the house or refuse to engage in activities they once enjoyed. In either case, it's important to respond with patience and understanding. If your pet is seeking more attention, offer it willingly, but if they are withdrawing, gently encourage interaction without forcing it. They will come to you when they are ready.

Pacing or Restlessness

Some pets may become more restless after losing a companion. Dogs, in particular, may start pacing around the house, walking from room to room as if they are looking for something—or someone—that is missing. They may appear anxious, unable to settle in one spot for long, or they might follow you closely as if they are seeking comfort. This behavior is often a sign of anxiety and uncertainty, and it's important to provide them with calming reassurance. Regular walks, playtime, or even new activities that engage their mind can help redirect this restlessness and give them a sense of purpose.

Easing Anxiety in Grieving Pets

Helping a pet through their grief is a process that requires patience and understanding. Each pet grieves in their own way, and it's important to provide them with the emotional and physical support they need to adjust to life without their companion. Here are some practical ways to ease their anxiety and help them cope:

Consistency Is Key

Pets thrive on routine, so maintaining a consistent schedule for feeding, walks, and playtime can provide them with a sense of security. For example, if your dog was used to going on a walk at a certain time each day with their companion, continue this routine. Even if you're now walking alone, the familiar activity can help ease the transition. Similarly, for cats, maintaining feeding times and quiet play sessions can offer comfort and stability.

Provide Extra Comfort

Whether it's through physical affection, quiet companionship, or simply spending more time together, offering extra comfort during this time can help ease your pet's anxiety. If they used to cuddle with their companion, they may now seek that closeness from you. Don't hesitate to spend a little extra time sitting with them, petting them, or even just being near them so they don't feel as alone. For pets who seem more withdrawn, giving them space while still being present can show that you're there for them when they're ready to engage.

Introduce New Toys or Activities

Providing your pet with new toys or engaging them in activities they enjoy can help divert their focus from the loss. For dogs, puzzle toys or interactive games can stimulate their minds and keep them occupied. Cats might enjoy exploring new spaces, playing with interactive toys, or watching the outside world from a cozy window perch. These activities can offer a healthy distraction and help reduce feelings of anxiety.

Use Familiar Scents

Pets rely heavily on their sense of smell, and sometimes, having something that still carries the scent of their lost companion can bring comfort. You might consider placing a blanket, bed, or toy that still smells like the other pet in their favorite spot. This can provide them with a sense of connection, even though their friend is no longer physically present.

Be Patient

Just like people, pets need time to grieve and adjust. Some might bounce back quickly, while others may need weeks or even months to fully recover from the loss. During this period, it's important to be patient and understanding, allowing your pet the space they need to process their feelings. If your pet's behavior doesn't improve over time, or if they continue to show signs of severe distress, consulting a veterinarian or an animal behaviorist can provide additional guidance.

Chapter 8:

Rediscovering Joy After Loss—

How to Move Forward

Losing a beloved pet can be one of the most challenging experiences, and it often leaves a void that feels almost impossible to fill. The bond that people share with their pets is so unique, filled with unconditional love, companionship, and countless joyful moments. When that bond is broken by loss, it can feel overwhelming, and sometimes it's hard to imagine being able to feel happiness again. Yet, even in the middle of grief, there is a way forward—a way to rediscover joy without ever diminishing the love or the memories of your pet.

Rediscovering happiness after such a loss is an essential part of the healing process. It's not about forgetting or replacing the deep connection that you had; instead, it's about finding a way to honor those memories while also making room for new moments of peace and joy. This journey takes time, and it looks different for everyone, but in time, it becomes possible to embrace the beautiful memories while still moving forward.

Honoring your pet's legacy can be a meaningful part of this process. Small acts of kindness, such as donating to animal shelters or participating in animal advocacy, can offer a sense of purpose and help keep the connection to the bond you shared alive. These acts not only keep the memory of your pet alive, but they also create opportunities for you to find fulfillment in new and unexpected ways. Eventually, you might even find yourself open to exploring new passions, or perhaps, in time, you may consider bringing another animal into your life.

Balancing those cherished memories with the possibility of new experiences is one of the keys to moving forward. You may find that talking about your pet's life in positive, uplifting ways—celebrating the joy they brought into your life rather than focusing only on the sadness of their loss—can be a powerful step toward healing. Shifting your perspective in this way allows you to hold on to the love while also making space for new sources of happiness.

Whether it's through volunteering, working in animal welfare, or taking up a new hobby, these small yet significant steps can help guide you toward rediscovering joy. This process doesn't mean forgetting the past; instead, it means acknowledging that life, even after loss, can still offer moments of joy that are worth treasuring.

Embracing Memories of Your Pet While Welcoming New Joy

When we lose a pet, it can sometimes feel like the memories are all we have left, and we might be scared of losing even those. But one of the most comforting things to remember is that the bond you had with your pet is never truly lost—it just takes on a new form. Instead of daily routines spent feeding or playing with your pet, you can find other ways to hold on to their presence in your life.

A gentle way to keep your pet's memory close is by creating small daily rituals. Perhaps every morning, you take a moment to reflect on a happy memory you shared—maybe the way your dog greeted you with a wagging tail when you came home or how your cat curled up in your lap on lazy afternoons. These moments of reflection can be healing, as they allow you to feel connected to your pet even though they're no longer physically there. You could also place a favorite photo of your pet in a spot where you'll see it often, such as on your desk or by your bed. Just seeing their face might bring a smile to yours, and over time, those memories can become a source of warmth rather than sadness.

Another meaningful way to embrace these memories is by keeping items that remind you of your pet. A collar, a favorite toy, or a clay paw print—having a tangible item can help you feel that your pet's presence still lingers in your home. Some people create a small memorial area—a corner of their room or garden where they place these items, offering a peaceful space to remember their beloved companion. This special place can become a sanctuary where you honor the love you shared.

As you hold on to these memories, it's also important to recognize that it's okay to make room for new joy. You don't have to rush the process, and it doesn't mean that you're forgetting or replacing your pet. The love you have for them doesn't disappear just because you open your heart to new experiences. If and when the time feels right, welcoming a new pet into your life can be a beautiful way to continue the cycle of love. It's a chance to give another animal the care and affection you have to offer while still cherishing the memories of the one you've lost.

Honoring Your Pet's Legacy Through Acts of Kindness or Animal Advocacy

One of the most heartfelt ways to honor your pet's memory is through acts of kindness. The love and joy they brought into your life can be shared with others, particularly with animals in need. Donating to an animal shelter or rescue in your pet's name is a thoughtful gesture that ensures their legacy lives on by helping other animals find the care and love they deserve. You might choose to donate food or toys or even make a monetary contribution to support veterinary care for animals awaiting adoption. Each act of kindness, no matter how small, becomes a way to pass on the compassion your pet inspired in you.

Volunteering your time is another deeply personal way to honor your pet's legacy. Spending time at a local animal shelter, helping walk dogs, or offering to foster animals in need can bring a sense of purpose during your grief. It allows you to stay connected to the world of animals while giving back to those who need it most. Many find that offering care to other pets, even temporarily, helps fill the space left by their own pet's passing. It doesn't take away the pain, but it channels that love into something positive, allowing it to grow and make a difference.

For those who are passionate about animal welfare, advocacy can be a powerful way to keep your pet's memory alive. You could become involved in campaigns promoting animal rights, raising awareness about adoption, or even helping educate others on responsible pet care. By advocating for the well-being of animals, you ensure that your pet's legacy is one of kindness and protection. It's a way of saying, "The love I shared with my pet was special, and I want other animals to experience that same care."

If your pet has a favorite activity or place, you might consider honoring them in a way that reflects their unique personality. For example, if your dog loved playing at the park, you could donate a bench with their name engraved on it or provide toys for other dogs to enjoy. If your cat had a favorite window where they spent their days, you might create a little memorial there with a small figurine or their favorite blanket. These personalized acts of kindness not only honor their memory but allow their spirit to live on in the joy of other animals.

For those who prefer quieter acts of remembrance, something as simple as writing a letter to your pet can be healing. In it, you might express your gratitude for the love they gave you and reflect on how they touched your life. You can tuck the letter away in a keepsake box or even include it in a larger memorial with their collar or a tuft of their fur. This simple act of writing can bring a sense of closure, helping you to process your emotions and honor the profound bond you shared.

Finding Joy Again

After losing a pet, one of the most challenging things to do is begin thinking about life beyond that loss. It's hard to imagine what your days will look like when they've been so full of the routines and love you shared with your pet. The grief can feel all-consuming at first, but slowly, thoughts about the future will start to emerge. You might wonder if you'll ever feel ready to welcome a new pet into your life or if there's a way to fill the void left behind. These are natural feelings, and everyone moves through them in their own time. There's no rush, and it's okay to take small steps, allowing yourself to process each moment as it comes.

Beginning to Think About Life After Loss

When you're ready to begin thinking about what comes next, it's important to start gently. You might not feel prepared to make any big decisions right away, and that's perfectly fine. The process of healing and moving forward looks different for everyone. Some people may find comfort in the idea of bringing a new pet into their lives, while others may feel they need more time before considering another animal companion.

If you do feel that getting another pet might help you heal, take some time to reflect on what you're ready for. The love you had for your previous pet will always be there, and getting another pet doesn't mean you're replacing that bond. Instead, it's a way to continue sharing the love and care you have to offer. Many people who've lost a pet find joy in rescuing an animal in need, knowing that their new companion is bringing fresh energy into their home while still honoring the memory of the pet they've lost.

On the other hand, if you feel that now is not the right time for another pet, that's okay, too. There are other ways to bring fulfillment and purpose into your life without committing to a new pet right away. You might begin exploring other interests that offer a sense of comfort and joy.

Suggestions for Volunteering, Animal Welfare Work, or New Hobbies

One wonderful way to stay connected to animals, even if you're not ready for a new pet, is through volunteering. Many animal shelters and rescue organizations are always looking for extra hands to help care for their animals. You could spend time walking dogs, helping to socialize cats, or simply providing companionship to animals that are waiting for their forever homes. Volunteering offers a meaningful way to give back, and you'll find that being around animals again can be incredibly soothing, even as you continue to process your grief.

In addition to working directly with animals, you might also explore ways to support animal welfare more broadly. This could involve advocating for better treatment of animals in your community or helping raise awareness about adoption and the importance of spaying and neutering pets. Many organizations host events like charity walks or fundraisers, and participating in these can help you stay involved in a cause that's close to your heart. It's a way of turning your grief into something positive, knowing that your efforts are helping improve the lives of other animals.

If working with animals feels too difficult at the moment or you're looking for something different, exploring new hobbies can be another avenue for healing. You could take up photography, focusing on capturing moments of beauty in nature or even documenting the lives of animals in shelters. Creative activities like writing, drawing, or gardening can also provide an emotional outlet, giving you a space to express your feelings while creating something new. Gardening, in particular, is a peaceful hobby, and some people choose to plant a memorial garden in honor of their pet, finding comfort in watching something grow and flourish as a tribute to their beloved companion.

How to Talk About Your Pet's Life in Positive and Uplifting Ways

As you move through your grief, talking about your pet's life can be an important part of healing. While it's natural to feel sadness when you think about the time you spent together, there is also great joy in remembering the happy moments. Sharing stories about your pet—whether it's with family, friends, or even in a journal—helps keep their memory alive in a way that feels uplifting. You might talk about the silly things your pet did that made you laugh or recall the quiet moments when they comforted you without saying a word. These memories are treasures, and they can bring a smile to your face, even during difficult times.

When you're ready, you could consider creating a photo album or a scrapbook filled with pictures of your pet. Looking through old photos and reflecting on the experiences you shared can be a bittersweet but ultimately rewarding way to remember them. You might find that putting your memories into words—whether it's by writing an obituary or simply recording your favorite stories—helps you celebrate your pet's life in a positive way. It allows you to focus on the good times, and over time, these memories can become a source of comfort rather than pain.

Another idea is to talk about your pet with others who know them well. Sharing memories with people who also loved your pet can help you feel less alone in your grief. They might recall moments you'd forgotten or offer their own reflections that add to your sense of connection with your pet's legacy. It's a way of keeping their spirit alive through shared stories and laughter.

Finding a Balance Between Holding on to Memories and Making Room for New Experiences

One of the most delicate parts of moving forward after loss is finding a balance between holding on to your pet's memory and making space for new experiences. It can feel like a tightrope at times—you want to honor your pet and the place they held in your life, but you also want to open yourself up to future joy. It's important to remember that these two things don't have to be in conflict. You can cherish the past while still embracing the future.

Allow yourself to hold on to the memories that bring you comfort. Whether it's through keeping their collar in a special place, planting a tree in their honor, or simply reflecting on your favorite moments together, these memories are part of your healing journey. They remind you of the love that never goes away, even after your pet is gone.

At the same time, making room for new experiences is an essential part of moving forward. This might mean taking up a new hobby, volunteering in a different capacity, or even traveling to places you've always wanted to visit. It could also mean, when the time is right, welcoming another pet into your life. Whatever form these new experiences take, they are not a replacement for the past but a continuation of your journey. You'll carry the memory of your pet with you as you create new moments of joy.

Chapter 9:

Finding Healing in New Companions (When You're Ready)

After the loss of a beloved pet, the grief can be overwhelming, leaving a space in your life that feels impossible to fill. The memories of your time together are precious, but they may also bring a deep sense of sadness as you adjust to life without your companion. In these moments, it is natural to wonder whether your heart could ever open again to welcome a new pet. Moving forward does not mean replacing the love you shared, but it might mean discovering that your heart has room for more than you imagined.

When the time is right, bringing a new companion into your life can be a powerful step in your journey of healing. However, this is not a decision to be taken lightly. It is important to reflect on your emotional readiness and to honor both your grief and the potential joy that a new pet might bring. Welcoming a new pet doesn't erase the love you had for your previous companion; rather, it can help you continue your legacy by sharing your love with another.

Before you begin considering adoption, there are some important questions to ask yourself. Are you truly ready to take on the responsibilities that come with a new pet? Do you have space in your heart and home to care for another animal while still cherishing the memory of the one you lost? These questions require thoughtful reflection because the decision to adopt should feel right for you, both emotionally and practically.

As you evaluate whether you are ready for this new chapter, personal stories from others who have gone through a similar journey can offer insight and comfort. They show that it's possible to hold on to the memory of your lost pet while finding joy and connection with a new companion. Each person's experience is unique, but the common thread is that love, in all its forms, has the power to heal.

Finding the right time to adopt a new pet is a deeply personal process, one that depends on your circumstances and emotional state. When you decide to welcome a new companion, the choice of which pet to bring into your home is equally significant. The bond you form with this new member of your family will be different, but that doesn't make it any less meaningful. As you move forward, you can take comfort in knowing that healing doesn't mean forgetting, and love only grows stronger when shared.

When And How to Consider Bringing a New Pet

When you lose a beloved pet, the grief can feel overwhelming, and the house that was once filled with their presence can suddenly seem empty. It's natural, at this point, to wonder when the right time might be to welcome a new pet into your home. This decision is deeply personal, and it's different for everyone. There's no strict timeline for when you should open your heart to another animal, but there are some important things to consider before you do. You'll want to reflect on your emotions, the state of your heart, and the practicalities of caring for a new pet. Let's explore how you can assess your readiness for this new chapter, the questions you should ask yourself, and how to make space in your heart for both the memory of your lost pet and the love for a new one.

When to Consider Bringing a New Pet Into Your Home

After a pet passes away, it's common to feel an intense sense of loss and emptiness. The routines you once shared with your pet, like feeding them or going on walks, can remind you of what is no longer there. In moments like these, it's tempting to want to fill that emptiness right away by bringing another pet into your life. However, it's really important to take a step back and evaluate if you are truly ready.

Grieving takes time, and everyone grieves in their own way. You may be asking yourself, "How long should I wait before adopting another pet?" The truth is, there is no right or wrong answer to that question. Some people feel ready to adopt within days, while others may take months or even years to heal. The key here is to give yourself the time and space you need to process your grief fully. If you bring home a new pet too soon, you may find it difficult to bond with them, as the emotional wounds from your previous loss might still feel too raw.

Take a moment to check in with yourself and your emotions. Are you still deeply mourning your pet, or have you begun to reach a place of peace and acceptance? If thinking about your lost pet still brings intense sadness or tears, it might be a sign that you're not quite ready. This isn't a race—you don't need to rush the decision. The love and memories you shared with your previous pet will always be a part of you, and whenever you're ready, a new pet will find a place in your heart without diminishing the bond you had with the one you lost.

Questions to Ask Yourself Before Adopting Another Pet

Deciding to adopt another pet is a big step, and it's not one to take lightly. There are a few questions you should ask yourself to make sure that you're truly ready, both emotionally and practically, to bring a new companion into your home.

Why Do I Want a New Pet?

This might be the most important question of all. Are you adopting because you genuinely want to welcome a new friend into your life, or are you hoping to fill the emptiness left by your previous pet's passing? While it's completely normal to feel lonely after losing a pet, adopting another animal just to ease the pain might not be the best reason. You want to be sure that your motivation comes from a place of love and readiness, not just a desire to make the sadness go away.

Am I Ready to Care for a New Pet Emotionally?

It's essential to consider where you are in your grieving process. Have you reached a point where you can think about your lost pet and smile at the memories, or does it still hurt too much? If your emotions are still raw, you might find it hard to connect with a new pet, and that can lead to feelings of guilt or frustration. It's okay to wait until you feel more settled and emotionally prepared to open your heart again.

Do I Have the Time and Energy for a New Pet?

A new pet, especially a young one, requires a lot of time and attention. You'll need to be ready to invest in their care, from training to exercise and even just spending time bonding. Think about your current lifestyle—are you able to provide the care and attention a new pet will need, or are you too busy right now? If you're unsure, fostering a pet can be a great way to see if you're ready without making a long-term commitment right away.

How Will a New Pet Affect My Other Pets?

If you already have pets at home, it's important to think about how they might react to a new addition. Pets can grieve the loss of a companion, too, and they may not be ready for another animal in the house just yet. Before adopting, take the time to observe how your other pets are coping. Are they adjusting well to the loss, or are they still showing signs of mourning? Bringing in a new pet too soon might upset the balance and cause unnecessary stress for your existing pets.

How to Ensure Your Heart Has Space for Both the Memory of Your Lost Pet and the Love for a New One

One of the hardest parts of considering a new pet is the fear that adopting again somehow diminishes the love you have for your lost pet. It's common to worry that welcoming a new pet into your home might feel like replacing the one you lost or, worse, betraying their memory. But it's important to remember that love doesn't work that way—your heart has room for both.

A New Pet Doesn't Replace Your Old Pet

Each pet we love is unique, with their own personality, quirks, and special place in our hearts. When you adopt a new pet, you're not replacing the one you lost because that love is irreplaceable. Instead, think of it as adding a new chapter to your life. The memories and bonds you shared with your old pet will always be a part of you, and no new pet can take that away. By welcoming a new pet into your home, you're not forgetting your previous companion—you're simply creating new memories alongside the ones you already hold dear.

Honoring the Memory of Your Lost Pet

One way to help ensure that your lost pet's memory remains an important part of your life is by honoring them in some special way. This could be as simple as keeping a favorite photo or toy in a meaningful place or creating a small memorial. These gestures can provide a sense of closure and help you feel like your old pet's memory is always with you, even as you move forward with a new companion.

Evaluating Your Emotional Readiness for a New Pet

When it comes to evaluating your emotional readiness, it's all about being honest with yourself. Ask yourself if you're ready to open your heart to a new pet without feeling weighed down by grief. Can you think about your lost pet without overwhelming sadness? Do you feel excitement at the idea of bringing home a new companion, or are you still hesitant and unsure?

It's okay if you're not quite ready yet. It's better to wait until you feel a sense of peace and clarity rather than rushing into something before your heart has fully healed. But if you find yourself feeling joyful at the thought of adopting again, and if the idea of a new pet brings a smile to your face, it might be a sign that you're ready to take that step.

How to Choose the Right Time and Pet

After a pet has passed, it's natural to feel a strong pull toward filling the space they left behind. However, bringing a new animal into your life is a decision that needs care and reflection, ensuring both you and your new pet are in the best possible situation to thrive together.

Taking Time to Reflect

The first step in deciding when to bring a new pet home is giving yourself time to reflect on your emotional state and the realities of your day-to-day life. Grief can take time, and rushing into a new relationship with a pet might seem like a solution to the heartache, but it's essential to make sure you're adopting for the right reasons. If you're still feeling the sharp sting of your loss, it may be wise to allow yourself more time. On the other hand, if you've reached a point where you feel ready for a new companion, that could be a signal that your heart is healing.

When you've lost a pet, the daily routines you once had may feel strangely empty. The walk you used to take or the quiet moments you shared can become reminders of what's missing. It's okay to acknowledge that feeling, but make sure you're adopting because you're ready to start a new chapter, not just because you want to fill that void quickly.

Practical Considerations

Aside from emotional readiness, it's also important to think about the practical aspects of adopting a new pet. Ask yourself if your current lifestyle is suited to the kind of pet you're considering. If you're looking at adopting a dog, for instance, do you have the time and energy for daily walks, training, and playtime? If you're considering a cat, think about whether your living space provides enough room for them to explore and be comfortable.

Also, take a close look at your schedule. Do you have time to bond with a new pet? Bringing home a young pet, like a puppy or a kitten, means taking on the added responsibilities of training, socializing, and making sure they feel secure in their new environment. If your life is currently hectic or you're adjusting to new work demands, it might be worth waiting until things settle down.

Older pets, on the other hand, might be a better fit for those who want companionship but may not have the energy for the extra care that young animals require. Many older pets are already trained and have a calmer demeanor, making them an excellent option for people who might not be up for the task of raising a younger pet but still want to share their home with a loyal companion.

Consider the Needs of Other Pets in the Home

If you already have pets, their needs must be taken into account as well. Pets can experience grief just like humans, and the loss of a companion might affect them in different ways. Some animals may become withdrawn or lose interest in their usual activities, while others might show signs of needing more attention and interaction. Before you bring a new pet into the mix, think about how it might impact the dynamics in your home. It's important to ensure that your existing pets are ready for a new companion, as introducing a new pet too soon could cause stress or conflict.

For instance, if you have an older dog who is used to a slower pace, adopting a rambunctious puppy might not be the best choice. In that case, a more mature, calmer pet could be a better fit. Observing your pets' behaviors and talking to your vet about their readiness can help guide you toward the best decision.

Moving Forward With Confidence

Moving forward with a new pet doesn't mean erasing the past. It's about finding a way to bring love and companionship into your life again while still holding on to the memories of your lost pet. Choosing the right time to adopt is as much about emotional readiness as it is about ensuring your home and lifestyle are suitable for a new animal.

Take the time you need to reflect, be honest with yourself about your motivations, and when you feel ready, open your heart to the possibilities a new pet can bring. Your new pet will create their own special place in your life, just as the one you lost will always hold a cherished spot in your heart.

Conclusion

As we come to the end of this book, I truly hope that the words you've read have brought you a little comfort and understanding during what is undoubtedly a difficult time. Losing a beloved pet is not just something that happens and passes—it's a deep, personal experience that touches the heart in a way many people might not expect. And that's why it's so important to remind yourself that the grief you are feeling is absolutely normal. It's a reflection of the love and joy you shared with your pet, and it's okay to let yourself feel that fully.

We've talked about a lot in this book. From the initial shock and heartbreak of losing a pet to the complex emotions of guilt and sadness that often follow, each chapter has hopefully served as a guide to help you navigate these difficult emotions. One thing I want to remind you of, though, is that grief is a journey. And, like any journey, it takes time, and it's rarely straightforward. There may be days when you feel like you're moving forward, only to have another day when a memory or a small reminder brings the sadness back. And, honestly, that's perfectly okay. This back-and-forth, this ebb and flow of emotions, is completely natural when you're grieving the loss of a pet who meant so much to you.

One of the things we touched on was how grief isn't linear. It doesn't follow a checklist, where once you've passed through one stage, you're done with it forever. No, it's a much more fluid and personal experience. Some days you might feel fine, and other days you might find yourself overwhelmed with sadness all over again. And it's important to remember that this is not a sign that you're "stuck" or not healing. Grief comes and goes in waves, and it's okay to let those feelings come without judgment. Allow yourself the space to cry when you need to, smile when you're reminded of a happy moment, or simply sit with your feelings, whatever they are. This is all part of the healing process.

We also spent time talking about ways to honor and memorialize your pet. Creating a lasting tribute to your pet, whether that's through something as simple as a photo album or as meaningful as planting a tree, can be a beautiful way to keep their memory alive. By finding ways to honor your pet, you're not only keeping their spirit with you, but you're also helping yourself heal. Memorializing your pet allows you to celebrate the life you shared together while also finding a way to move forward. It doesn't have to be elaborate or complicated—what matters is that it feels right to you and helps you hold on to the love you feel.

And then there's the practical side of pet loss, which we discussed as well. Handling the logistics after your pet passes can feel overwhelming, especially when emotions are running high. Whether it's deciding between cremation or burial, talking to children or other loved ones about what happens next, or just figuring out what steps you need to take, it can feel like too much at times. But as we talked about in the book, taking things one step at a time and allowing yourself to lean on others for support can help make these moments more manageable. Don't hesitate to ask for help when you need it and remember that you're not alone in this.

One of the hardest aspects of losing a pet, for many people, is dealing with the feelings of guilt that can arise, particularly if you have to make the decision to euthanize your pet. This is such a heavy burden to carry, and it's easy to second-guess yourself or feel like you could have done more. But it's important to remind yourself that choosing euthanasia, while heartbreaking, is often an act of love. It's a way to prevent unnecessary suffering, and though the decision is painful, it's made out of care and compassion. Letting go of that guilt isn't easy, but it's an important part of the healing process. Your pet felt your love every day of their life, and in the end, you made the kindest choice you could.

We also talked about the importance of supporting your family and other pets through this time. Grieving isn't something that happens in isolation, and the loss of a pet can impact everyone in your home, including your other animals. By coming together, sharing stories, and comforting each other, you help everyone in your family—including your surviving pets—find their way forward. Children, especially, may need extra guidance as they process their emotions, and pets may show signs of grief that you didn't expect. But by recognizing these needs and addressing them with care, you can help create a supportive environment for healing.

One of the most important things to remember is that rediscovering joy after loss is not about replacing your pet or moving on without them. It's about allowing yourself to live fully again while still holding on to the love and memories of your pet. Whether it's through new hobbies, volunteering with animals, or simply finding moments of happiness in your everyday life, joy will return in time. For some, this might also mean welcoming a new pet into the home. This doesn't mean that you're forgetting your lost pet—it's simply a way to make room in your heart for new love and new experiences. And when you're ready, you'll know it's time to open your heart again.

So, as we bring this book to a close, I want to leave you with this: Your journey through grief is personal, and there's no right or wrong way to navigate it. Healing will come, not all at once, but gradually, with time, patience, and compassion for yourself. The love you shared with your pet will always be a part of you, and their memory will live on in your heart. You've made it through this far, and you will continue to find your way, little by little, step by step. And when the time comes, you'll rediscover joy, knowing that the love you had for your pet will always be a part of who you are.

Take care of yourself, and remember: The love you shared was real, and that love will guide you as you move forward.

Dear Reader!

Thank you for giving my book a place in your life! I truly hope it brought you peace, healing and comfort.

If you enjoyed this book, I would be honored if you would share your experience in a quick review. Reviews are one of the most helpful ways to support independent authors, and your feedback helps others decide if this book might be right for them.

How to leave a review:

1. Scan the QR code below, and it will take you straight to my book

OR - follow this URL address: www.amazon.com/dp/B0D97JMTM

2. Scroll down to the "Write a Customer Review" section.

3. Share your honest thoughts and rate the book.

Thank you so much for your support!

With my deepest gratitude,

Natalie Harlow

References

Arora, A., Clarida, R., Maria, R., Forero, L., Steffan, B., & Zamora, V. (2020). *Pet loss best practice guidelines for veterinary teams*. VCA Animal Hospitals. https://www.senecapolytechnic.ca/content/dam/projects/seneca/schools/school-of-health-science/pet-loss-best-practice-guidelines-for-veterinary-teams.pdf

Blue Cross. (n.d.). *"Goodbye my friend": A story of pet loss*. Blue Cross. https://www.bluecross.org.uk/story/goodbye-my-friend-a-story-of-pet-loss

Brennan, J. (n.d.). *Service animals and emotional support animals*. ADA National Network. https://adata.org/guide/service-animals-and-emotional-support-animals

Buzby, J. (2020, July 10). Grieving the loss of a dog after euthanasia (& finding peace). Dr. Buzby's ToeGrips. https://toegrips.com/grieving-the-loss-of-dog-after-euthanasia/

Cummings School of Veterinary Medicine. (n.d.). *Pet loss support helpline*. Cummings School of Veterinary Medicine. https://vet.tufts.edu/pet-loss-support-helpline

Holland, K. (2024, September 30). *The stages of grief and what to expect*. Healthline. https://www.healthline.com/health/stages-of-grief

Kessler, C. (2021, September 24). *What you need to know about pet burial and cremation*. Funeral Basics. https://www.funeralbasics.org/pet-burial-and-cremation/

Smith, M., Robinson, L., & Segal, J. (2024, October 23). *Coping with grief and loss: Stages of grief and how to heal*. HelpGuide.org.

https://www.helpguide.org/mental-health/grief/coping-with-grief-and-loss

Wein, H. (2018, February). *The power of pets*. NIH News in Health. https://newsinhealth.nih.gov/2018/02/power-pets